Fife Coastal Path

Sandra Bardwell
and Jacquetta Megarry

Rucksack Readers

Fife Coastal Path

First published in 2015, reprinted with minor revisions in 2018, by Rucksack Readers,
6 Old Church Lane, Edinburgh, EH15 3PX, UK

Telephone +44/0 131 661 0262

Email info@rucsacs.com, website *www.rucsacs.com*

British Library cataloguing in publication data: a catalogue record for this book is
available from the British Library.

ISBN 978-1-898481-71-3

Designed in Scotland by Ian Clydesdale (*www.workhorse.scot*).

Printed in Poland by Pario Print of Kraków on waterproof, biodegradable paper from
FSC sources.

Title page photograph: St Monans Church from the west

Publisher's note

Long-distance routes are constantly evolving. Three route improvements were made to the Fife Coastal
Path in 2015 alone, and further changes are inevitable. Follow local signage carefully, and before setting
out check two websites for updates:
www.fifecoastalpath.co.uk and *www.rucsacs.com/books/fcp*.

Parts of the route are wet underfoot, others rough and rocky. Navigation is generally straightforward,
and waymarking clear and consistent. You are responsible for making sure that your clothing, food and
equipment are suited to your needs, and that you can complete your intended walk safely given the
hours of daylight and state of the tide. The publisher cannot accept any liability for any ill-health, injury
or loss arising directly or indirectly from reading this book.

Feedback is welcome and will be rewarded

All feedback will be followed up, and readers whose comments lead to changes will be entitled to claim a
free copy of our next edition upon publication. Please send emails to **info@rucsacs.com**.

Contents

Introduction

'A beggar's mantle fringed wi' gowd' – the 'gowd' in King James VI of Scotland's description of Fife referred to the value of trade through its coastal ports. Modern walkers may strike gold of another kind when they discover the coastal scenery of Fife.

The Kingdom of Fife derives from the Pictish Kingdom of Fib. Defying all changes in governance, the label Kingdom has persisted ever since. Sandwiched between the Firths of Forth and Tay, Fife is more island than peninsula, and many Fifers speak of their Kingdom with patriotic pride.

Fife's role in Scottish history is attested by churches, castles and caves with ancient carvings. The villages of its East Neuk (corner) have charming whitewashed cottages and they host arts festivals. The ancient university town of St Andrews was once Scotland's ecclesiastic capital, and is famous worldwide as the home of golf.

For the walker, this is a route of contrasts. Easy, flat walking through dunes and beside golf courses often leads to slow going on rocky shorelines. Clifftop paths afford wide views, disused railway trackbed is more secluded; in the north there's some forest, and the final section is largely farmland. Urban walking is inevitable, some of it uninspiring.

The Path runs through several nature reserves, with great chances to sight seabirds, seals and dolphins. The villages have welcoming pubs, famous fish-and-chip shops and good B&Bs. Whether you opt for the original bridge-to-bridge route (81 miles/131 km) or commit to the extended route (117 miles/187 km), the Fife Coastal Path awaits you.

Kincraig Point

1 Planning

Best time of year and weather

The ideal time to walk the Fife Coastal Path is between May and September. In Scotland, hours of daylight are long in summer, especially during late May to late July. Also, there is a better chance of good weather, and more flexibility within each day, for the 6-10 days that most people will need to complete the route. If you to want to visit the Isle of May, boats run only from April to September inclusive: see page 24. Be aware also of various arts festivals held in the East Neuk in July/August: see www.rucsacs.com/links/fcp.

Winter is better avoided, at least if planning to complete the route in a single expedition, because poor weather is more likely and short days are certain. But if you live within striking distance and wish to complete the route in sections, you could set off at short notice, whenever the immediate weather forecast is favourable. It is vital to make best use of the very limited daylight hours on such winter forays.

The weather in Scotland is highly variable. Statistically, the best months are May and September but periods of good or bad weather can occur at any time of year. Conditions can change so quickly that you feel you're experiencing all four seasons in one day. The route is walkable in all weathers: the important thing is to be prepared. Check the weather forecast and tidal data for wherever you plan to walk: see page 78. Always carry appropriate clothing and equipment.

Which direction?

This guidebook is written for walkers heading anti-clockwise around the route. There are two good reasons why we recommended this direction. First, it means that you move from the more urban former mining towns on the Forth, through the charming fishing villages of the East Neuk, onward through historic St Andrews to reach the rural shores of the Firth of Tay beyond Newport. Second, it puts the prevailing wind (south-westerly) at your back for most of the Path, heading into the wind only on the final section – if you choose to include it: see below.

Most people will need to complete their route in a single expedition – unless you happen to live so close to Fife that day walks or weekend forays are feasible. That would allow you to pick and choose the most scenic sections, but we still recommend an anti-clockwise trend.

Which route: original or extended?

The Fife peninsula faces east, shaped like a dog's head: see map opposite. There are bridges at only two points – south across the Forth and north across the Tay. When officially opened in 2003, the Path ran for 81.4 miles/131 km from North Queensferry (at the Forth bridges) to Newport-on-Tay. This original bridge-to-bridge route is still what many or most people mean by the FCP. In 2011/12 the route was officially extended at both ends to encompass the entire Kingdom, adding 35.1 miles/56.5 km to its length and bringing a raft of logistic problems for unsupported walkers.

Most if not all tour operators still operate the original route, sending clients from North Queensferry to Newport, despite their awareness of the extensions and willingness to use vehicle transfers where necessary. Their decision is partly based on the need to tailor total distance and time to suit what most clients can spare. Mainly, however, it is to solve the problems of transport, compounded by lack of accommodation, at each end of the extended route.

In Parts 3.1 and 3.9, we describe the extensions in full detail, so that you can decide for yourself whether they justify the extra time and effort. As of 2018, there was no accommodation (other than possible airbnb options) at the official start, and at the Newburgh end only the 3-bedroom Abbey Inn which doesn't offer evening meals (albeit there is a Chinese take-away nearby). With nowhere to stay, walkers from afar may understandably be baffled as to how to reach Kincardine early enough to walk 17 miles (27 km) to North Queensferry. And unless booked into the Abbey Inn, you may find it hard to enjoy the final stretch of 18.3 miles (29.5 km) without anxiety about missing the last bus from Newburgh.

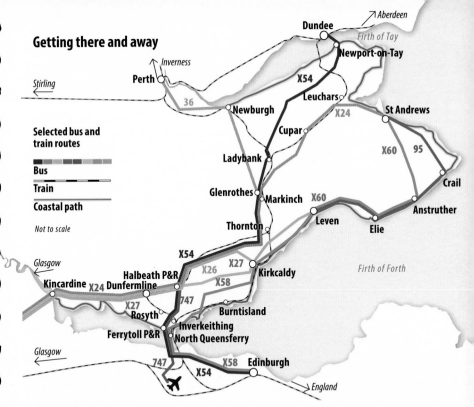

Getting there and away

Selected bus and train routes

Bus

Train

Coastal path

Not to scale

Access to Fife is much easier for the original bridge-to-bridge route than for the extended. North Queensferry, near Edinburgh, can be reached by rail or bus from Glasgow, Edinburgh or Perth: see page 79. Newport is opposite Dundee, and if ending your walk there, you can cross the road bridge and take a bus or train from Dundee. Indeed, many people overnight in Dundee for a much wider choice of accommodation.

Another option, caused by market forces in St Andrews B&Bs (see page 9), is to spend two nights there, walking to Newport on the second day and taking a local bus (route 99) back to St Andrews for the second night. This makes for a long last day, but smooths the return journey home – by bus from St Andrews or by train from Leuchars. To reach the official start at Kincardine means taking a bus, perhaps from Glasgow or Dunfermline or from Halbeath Park & Ride. To return from Newburgh, the only option is a bus. Stagecoach's route 36 runs between Glenrothes and Perth. As of 2018, the last bus to Glenrothes left at 19.45 (earlier on Sundays). Northbound, the last bus to Perth left Newburgh at 18.20 (earlier on Sundays). Perth has plenty of accommodation and good train and bus services, so will suit most people better than Glenrothes. However, if you miss the last bus, you face an expensive taxi ride to avoid being benighted in Newburgh. Contact details for public transport are on page 79. Timetables vary by the day and season: check carefully in advance.

How long will it take?

How many days you need to complete the entire route varies from person to person, and depends also on the size of your group and the distance you have to travel. Our route description is divided into nine sections, each of which can be completed in a single day by a fit hiker. However, if you are tackling the route in sections and need to allow some travel time, or if you prefer shorter distances, you may need to split some. Know your own strengths and weaknesses, and plan accordingly.

As explained above, omitting either the first and/or the final section of the official route may be preferable or necessary – especially if you have a long journey. Table 1a shows sample itineraries based on the exact sections in this book, with both extensions intact (16·8 miles/27 km and 18·3 miles/29·5 km): if you are following the bridge-to-bridge route you can simply ignore them for a 7-day itinerary, or reduce it to 6 days by skipping Leuchars. Table 1b shows different options for overnight stops, including Kingsbarns which is slightly offroute, so the overall distance is fractionally greater, but the longest section is only 16·3 miles (26·2 km). Although you can save a day by skipping St Andrews, this would be a shame unless you already know the town. You can pick and mix from either list: obviously there isn't space to list all the permutations. Read also pages 24 and 46-7 to decide whether you need extra overnights to visit the Isle of May or to complete the Elie Chainwalk at a safe state of the tide.

Table 1a 9-day itinerary based on guidebook sections

	miles	km	
Kincardine			
	16·8	27·0	
North Queensferry			
	11·8	19·0	
Burntisland			
	16·5	26·6	
Leven			
	9·6	15·4	
Elie			
	11.0	17·7	
Crail			
	13·3	21·4	
St Andrews			
	6·6	10·6	
Leuchars			19·2 30·9
	12·6	20·3	
Newport			
	18·3	29·5	
Newburgh			
Total	116·5	187·5	

1b 10-day itinerary based on alternative overnights

	miles	km	
Kincardine			
	11·5	18·5	
Limekilns			
	13·6	21·9	
Aberdour			
	12·0	19·3	
Dysart			
	10·5	16·9	
Lundin Links			
	10·9	17·5	
Anstruther			
	13·8	22·2	
*Kingsbarns			
	8·4	13·5	
St Andrews			15·0 24·1
	6·6	10·6	
Leuchars			
	15·0	24·1	
Wormit			
	16·3	26·2	
Newburgh			
Total	117·7	189·2	

*As of 2015, no evening meals were available

Accommodation and refreshments

You are seldom very far from a café, pub or shop, although your options become sparser beyond St Andrews. In the final stretch beyond Wormit there are no facilities until you reach Newburgh, where there are pub meals at weekends only. We show most options in the table below, focusing on places where in 2015 there was accommodation. Further refreshment options are shown on the map pages in Part 3.

With the sole exception of a basic dormitory hostel in St Andrews, Fife has no low-cost accommodation near the route, so unless you wish to camp (see page 10) you have to pay the price for B&Bs or hotels. Accommodation is available at all the overnight stops suggested in the tables on page 8. Larger places offer a selection, particularly towns such as Inverkeithing, Kirkcaldy, Leven and St Andrews. However, during golfing events and university graduation, most places in eastern Fife are fully booked months in advance; and many B&Bs in St Andrews impose a two-night minimum stay year-round. Smaller villages have very limited options, sometimes only a single B&B, which may be fully booked long in advance.

	miles from last place	km from last place	B&B/ hotel	campsite	pub	café	food shop/ carryout
Kincardine					✓	✓	✓
Culross	4·1	6·6	✓		✓	✓	✓
Limekilns	7·4	11·9	✓		✓	✓	✓
Rosyth	2·0	3·2	✓		✓	✓	✓
N Queensferry	3·3	5·3	✓		✓	✓	✓
Inverkeithing	2·5	4·0	✓		✓	✓	✓
Dalgety Bay	2·1	3·4			✓	✓	✓
Aberdour	3·6	5·8	✓		✓	✓	✓
Burntisland	3·6	5·8	✓		✓	✓	✓
Kinghorn	2·9	4·7	✓		✓	✓	✓
Kirkcaldy	3·0	4·8	✓	✓	✓	✓	✓
Dysart	2·5	4·0	✓				
West Wemyss	2·2	3·5			✓		✓
Buckhaven	3·2	5·1			✓	✓	✓
Methil	1·6	2·6			✓	✓	✓
Leven	1·1	1·8	✓		✓	✓	✓
Lower Largo	2·7	4·3	✓		✓	✓	✓
Elie	6·9	11·1	✓		✓	✓	✓
St Monans	3·3	5·3	✓	✓	✓	✓	✓
Pittenweem	1·8	2·9	✓		✓	✓	✓
Anstruther	1·7	2·7	✓		✓	✓	✓
Crail	4·0	6·4	✓	✓	✓	✓	✓
St Andrews	13·3	21·4	✓	✓	✓	✓	✓
Guardbridge	5·0	8·0	✓		✓	✓	✓
Leuchars	1·6	2·6	✓		✓	✓	✓
Tayport	10·0	16·1	✓		✓	✓	✓
Newport	3·0	4·8	✓		✓	✓	✓
Wormit	2·3	3·7	✓		✓	✓	✓
Newburgh	16·0	25·7	✓		✓	✓	✓

Details of accommodation can be obtained in various ways: see page 78. In all cases you need to book well in advance, especially in smaller places; for groups it is essential. Some people prefer to use a tour operator to book their accommodation and baggage transfer as a package. As of 2018, at least eight tour operators offered this route, and nearly all included baggage handling: see *www.rucsacs.com/books/fcp*.

Camping is, of course, the ultimate low-cost and self-reliant option for overnighting, but it still needs a bit of planning. Commercial campsites are shown on our mapping pages and in the table on page 9. They are sparse enough to make it impossible to do a full expedition without resorting to wild camping (or occasional B&Bs). Although wild camping is allowed in Scotland under the Scottish Outdoor Access Code (see below), parts of the Fife Coastal Path pass through farmland and urban areas with few if any suitable sites.

Cyclists and the Fife Coastal Path

The FCP was designed as a walking route. Under the SOAC, access rights extend to responsible cycling. So although route sections on hard surfaces and roads may be cycled, in narrow sections or where the path is wet and muddy, please avoid making it worse by cycling on it: dismount and walk until the path becomes suitable again. Many stretches of the FCP are unsuitable for bikes of any kind, notably the parts that run on beaches, the long sections from Fife Ness to St Andrews and all offroad sections from Wormit to Newburgh – although suitable quiet roads run in parallel. Keen cyclists would do better to focus on the Kingdom Cycle Route, a circuit of 105 miles/169 km. This runs along or near the FCP between North Queensferry and Kirkcaldy, then heads inland via Glenrothes. It returns to the coast (or nearby) from St Andrews to Newburgh, then reverts inland via Kinross and Dunfermline to end at North Queensferry.

In places the Path is shared with this cycleway, and sharing demands consideration from all users. Cyclists are rightly concerned about walkers who change direction abruptly without notice, or whose dogs stray into the path of an oncoming bike. And walkers are understandably indignant when cyclists whisk past without warning, sometimes at excessive speed.

Commonsense and courtesy are your best friends. Cyclists should notify their approach politely and in good time, whether by bell or voice, to allow walkers time to react. Walkers should look behind before making an unexpected move on shared sections. All users should stay in single file when they see oncoming walkers or cyclists.

The Scottish Outdoor Access Code

Under the Scottish Outdoor Access Code (SOAC), everyone has the statutory right to access to land for recreational purposes. Access rights must be exercised responsibly. They apply to most land in Scotland, including that which is privately owned, with the exceptions of gardens, farmyards and cultivated crops. For a summary of the Code, see page 11. For full details of the Code, including leaflets for dog owners and cyclists, please visit *www.outdooraccess-scotland.com*.

Everyone has the right to be on most land and inland water providing they act responsibly. Your access rights and responsibilities are explained fully in the Scottish Outdoor Access Code.

KNOW THE CODE BEFORE YOU GO
outdooraccess-scotland.com

Whether you're in the outdoors or managing the outdoors, the key things are to
- **take responsibility for your own actions** • **respect the interests of other people** • **care for the environment.**

Find out more by visiting *www.outdooraccess-scotland.com* or by contacting Scottish Natural Heritage; see page 78 for details.

Terrain and gradients

The route uses a mixture of footpaths, beaches, tracks and cycleways, and includes some stretches of minor road. A special feature is that it skirts and crosses so many golf courses. Keep to the marked path, and try to avoid spoiling golfers' concentration. Watch out for errant golf balls, and keep any dogs under very close control.

The route is generally low-level, with mostly gentle gradients and no serious climbs. It reaches its highest point about 7 miles (11 km) short of Newburgh on the shoulder of Norman's Law: even this is only about 260 m (850 ft) above sea level. Those who seek steeper terrain will find it in side-trips and, above all, if they choose to try the Elie Chainwalk: see pages 46-7.

Nevertheless, in many places the terrain is challenging and you will need stout footwear, especially during or after wet weather. Conditions underfoot vary also according to the tides. For beach walking, many people favour crocs or river sandals (as an alternative to walking boots), and tide awareness is vital: see page 13.

Waymarking and navigation

The Fife Coastal Path has dedicated waymarking, with a wavy blue/yellow/green logo representing sea, beach and hills. There's a variety of styles for these, typically fingerposts in rural stretches and stickers on street furniture in towns, where you need to be vigilant. If planning to stick to the route, you are unlikely to need to use your map and compass, except in very poor visibility in the last section from Newport to Newburgh.

⚠ Note that none of the map pages has North pointing up the page! The orientation of each page varies greatly as the route passes around the peninsula, and map pages are designed to be read from the bottom upwards. Each map has a North arrow that will help if you are using a compass. Each map also has red numerals along the route line to show mileage from Kincardine: subtract 17 if starting from North Queensferry, and refer to the inside back cover for miles/km conversion.

Remoteness and experience

Parts of the route in the north are surprisingly remote, and mobile phone reception can be patchy. GPS systems will not always work. However, waymarking is excellent, and if you have never done a long walk before, the Fife Coastal Path is a good choice. Ideally go with somebody who has more experience, and, above all, make realistic decisions about how far you should walk in a day. Please refer to our *Notes for novices*: see page 78.

Many people find they average no more than 2-2·5 mph (3-4 kph) over a full day, allowing for pauses and stops, although walkers vary widely. Solo walkers are likely to make faster time, and larger groups tend to move more slowly, but there is no substitute for experience in deciding what pace you find comfortable. If you haven't got time to stop and look at wildlife, views and points of interest, you have set yourself too great a distance goal to get the most from the route.

Credit and debit cards are generally accepted at hotels and larger shops, but small village shops usually prefer cash and some B&Bs do not accept cards of any kind. However cash machines (ATMs) are fairly widespread and some shops will provide cashback along with a purchase.

Tide awareness

Throughout a coastal walk, it is helpful to tune in to the time of high tide. There are two high tides daily, nearly 12½ hours apart, with two low tides in between. So high tide tomorrow will be about an hour later than today's. On this route there are several beaches where route choice may be determined by the state of the tide, and two places where the Path is unlikely to be passable safely at high tide. Also, do not embark on the Elie Chainwalk without precise tidal information: see page 47.

Ideally, plan ahead using *www.tides4fishing.com*. Failing that, you may find tide times from local newspapers and information boards. Be aware that the height of high tide varies: high tide is higher, and low tide lower, shortly after each full and new moon, especially about the time of the spring and autumn equinoxes. Remember that the weather, especially the wind, also affects wave height and force.

Leven beach

Responsible access and dogs

The route of the Fife Coastal Path has been negotiated with land managers and owners and it is important to respect their rights and maintain their goodwill. Use gates and stiles wherever provided, and leave gates as you find them, open or shut. Be sure to avoid causing any damage or making excessive noise in large groups.

If you want to take a dog along, think through all the practicalities. It must be kept under proper control at all times, with particular care when near livestock. Never allow your dog to approach sheep or cows that are, or may be, pregnant or with young. Coming between cattle and their young is dangerous, especially with a dog. You would also have to ask all your B&B hosts whether they accept dogs, and if any do not then you need to rethink. Having a dog with you also sharply limits your options for an evening meal.

Packing checklist

Assuming you are tackling the whole route in a single expedition, you may need most or all of what we list below. Opinions will differ as to what is essential and what is desirable, but this is a starting point for those in doubt. Adapt the list according to whether you are carrying for yourself or using a baggage service. Some items may be unnecessary if you are going in good weather and/or omitting the more remote parts of the route.

Essential
- rucksack (e.g 25-35 litres)
- waterproof rucksack cover or liner(s)
- comfortable walking boots and/or shoes
- specialist walking socks
- waterproof jacket and overtrousers
- clothing in layers (tops, trousers, jacket)
- hats for warmth and sun protection
- gloves
- guidebook with maps
- water carrier and plenty of water
- food for the more remote sections
- first aid kit, including blister treatment
- toilet tissue (biodegradable)
- overnight kit including toiletries
- insect repellent, sun protection (summer)

Desirable
- walking poles
- spare socks
- gaiters
- plastic bag(s) for litter
- camera and spare memory card
- spare batteries or charger for camera
- binoculars (useful for wildlife)
- notebook and pen
- pouch or secure pockets for keeping small items handy and safe
- mobile phone.

For campers
The above list assumes that you are using B&Bs. If you are camping, you'll also need a tent, sleeping gear, cooking utensils, portable stove, fuel and food, and a much larger rucksack to carry it all.

2 2·1 Geology and mining

Fife's landscape has evolved during a dramatically varied, overlapping sequence of geological eras. About 415 million years ago, the area was a desert with scant vegetation, and a hot semi-arid climate. Volcanoes reared up into this wilderness and ejected large quantities of molten material

Largo Law

from deep within the earth. Some of the material produced by their eruptions has resisted erosion, and survives in features such as the low cliff-edged ridges above Burntisland and Kirkcaldy in the east and near Newburgh in the north.

Many small volcanoes were scattered across Fife, of which Largo Law (see photo above) is a worn-down remnant. Other volcanic features include a dyke (rib of rock) at Elie harbour, and a stack of pillows of hard volcanic glass at the far end of Kinghorn Bay. At Ruby Bay, small red garnets, known as 'Elie rubies', may be found: these are fragments of magma embedded in outcrops of volcanic rock.

From one extreme to the other – about 100 million years later, Fife experienced a hot, humid climate and was largely covered by luxuriant vegetation. With fluctuating sea levels, sedimentary materials were laid down, forming strata of calcium-rich limestone, sandstone and mudstone.

Eventually the vegetation died and decomposed, forming thick beds of peat. This in turn was squashed by overlying sediments and turned into coal, occurring in seams up to 10 feet (3 m) thick. Then, major upheavals in the earth's crust distorted the layers of sedimentary rocks. This process is clearly illustrated at Maiden Rock, just past Kinkell Ness, approaching St Andrews.

During the last two million years a series of ice ages occurred. Lower areas around the Firths of Forth and Tay and the Eden estuary were inundated by east-flowing ice. Eventually it thawed, leaving behind huge deposits of gravel and sand.

Volcanic dykes near Fife Ness

From about 15,000 years ago, raised beaches were formed by the retreat of the ice, changes in sea levels and upheavals in the earth's crust. Later, with the slow increase in sea level and crustal movements, tiers of slightly tilted raised beaches were formed. They are now a few metres above sea level, notably at Kincraig near Elie. Near Boarhills (5 miles/8 km east of St Andrews) look out for Buddo Rock, made of pink sandstone and once part of the cliffs along a raised beach.

Perhaps the most striking features of Fife's entire coastline is the dramatic section between Fife Ness and St Andrews, where relatively recent erosion has attacked weaknesses in the rocks. The result is a fine collection of caves, arches, stacks and geos (deep, narrow inlets). A magnificent stack, the Rock & Spindle, stands about 2 miles

Rock & Spindle

(3 km) east of St Andrews – a tall pinnacle above a large boulder with an unusual radial pattern caused by cooling of volcanic rock.

Lime industry

Extensive limestone deposits around Charlestown and Limekilns brought considerable prosperity to Fife. Indeed Fife was the major supplier of lime to the entire UK, and it was widely exported. Lime was a key product in the building industry, and also used as a fertiliser, especially of barley crops used in whisky making.

Although small-scale production came earlier, it was in the 18th century that the industry really took off. Charles, Earl of Elgin sponsored the construction of a village at Charlestown which was completed in 1761. He greatly expanded the existing hamlet, and provided houses, a school and other facilities.

Raised beaches near Elie

Kilns were built in which quarried limestone was burned at a high temperature to make quicklime (calcium oxide). Water was then added to produce slaked lime (calcium hydroxide) – a basic building material and fertiliser. A small railway linked the pits where the limestone was quarried to the kilns, and the harbour was improved.

Production continued until the 1950s, and the kilns were closed in 1956. They stand near the old harbour, close to the FCP, and are being restored. The Scottish Lime Centre in Charlestown celebrates and promotes the knowledge and skills needed to conserve historic buildings: *www.scotlime.org*.

Coal mining

During the 19th and early 20th centuries Fife's coal mining industry was among the largest in Scotland and brought prosperity to the area. Mining may date back to the 13th century, and was certainly established around Dysart by the 1600s. The industry gradually expanded during the 19th century. Many pits were clustered around Kirkcaldy, Methil and Wemyss and there were more at Leven and Buckhaven. Some were very deep, for example 1565 feet/477 m near Methil.

Production was dominated by two companies – Wemyss Coal Company and the Fife Coal Company, which was once the largest in Scotland. Ports were built to ship the output to British and near European ports – West Wemyss in the early 16th century, Dysart (1831), Methil (about 1900) and Burntisland. Methil was at one time Scotland's busiest coal-exporting port, in 1904 shipping about six million tons of coal.

Winding gear, Frances colliery

Thousands of people were employed in the industry. They included women and children, although in 1842 children under 10 years of age were banned from working underground. However, large numbers of women and children continued to toil above ground for long hours and in poor conditions. Later in the 19th century things improved dramatically, with better safety provisions, more pay and shorter hours.

Pit closures happened from time to time, usually for economic reasons, but after World War 1 Fife's coal industry began to decline overall. By the late 1960s closures had accelerated, and by the end of the 1980s very few pits were still active. The last deep mine in Fife, Longannet near Culross, closed in 2002.

2·2 Economy: past and present

Industries such as mining, linen production, ship-building, salt production and brick manufacturing have traditionally been important to Fife's economy. So too were fishing, linoleum and golf, as explained below. Of the three, fishing has evolved into a much leaner, less visible venture, linoleum has almost disappeared, and golf has developed from the elite sport of royalty to the basis of a multi-million pound industry with lucrative media coverage of major tournaments.

Fishing

From about the 13th century, possibly earlier, fishing was the mainstay of the economy of villages and small towns in the East Neuk (eastern corner) of Fife. Anstruther and Pittenweem began as fishing villages. Ports were built and later expanded both there and at Crail. Elie and Burntisland also became important fishing towns. Anstruther, Pittenweem and Crail grew to be among the busiest fishing ports in Scotland. The main catch was herring during the winter and spring. It was salted and exported to the rest of Britain and to Europe.

The later 19th century was a time of great change in the industry. The arrival of the railways meant that the catch could be transported more safely and quickly. Sail power gave way to steam, then to diesel- and petrol-powered engines. The very long lines used to catch the fish were replaced by trawling and seine netting.

The industry thrived and at the peak of the herring boom around 1907, millions of barrels were sent to eastern Europe, Russia and Germany. However, both world wars depressed the industry and stocks dwindled so that herring had been virtually exhausted by the late 1940s.

Boat owners turned to whitefish and shellfish, upgraded to larger boats and introduced technical innovations. A side-effect was that fewer fishermen were needed. Fishing boats still operate in the area, mainly from Pittenweem.

The Scottish Fisheries Museum in Anstruther occupies several restored historic buildings on the harbour. Its extensive collection is of national significance and includes 19 original and model boats, equipment, photos and artworks. It is open daily all year: *www.scotfishmuseum.org*.

Anstruther harbour

Linoleum

Within living memory, Kirkcaldy was still the world's linoleum manufacturing capital, and had been for about a century. The industry continued to thrive until after World War 2, when new products and changing fashions precipitated a long-term decline. Today just one company, Swiss-owned Forbo Nairn, remains in production in Kirkcaldy.

The manufacturing process was invented by an Englishman, Frederick Walton, during the early 19th century using linen (or flax) and linseed oil. These constituents explain its name – 'linum' (Latin for linen) and 'oleum' (Latin for oil). After Walton's patent expired in 1876, it was taken up by John Nairn of Kirkcaldy. His business boomed almost straight away and the flooring material soon found markets throughout Britain and in overseas. It was judged to be high quality and won awards at several international exhibitions.

By the late 19th century six factories in Kirkcaldy employed about 3000 people directly or indirectly. Employees were treated very well by the owner who also endowed various local parks and public buildings. A factory was also established at Newburgh by the Tayside Floorcloth Company; it closed in 1980 after a disastrous fire.

The Kirkcaldy Museum & Art Gallery (gifted by John Nairn) has an exhibition about the industry. It includes samples, pattern books, tools and printing equipment. It's open daily, for variable hours: tel 01592 583 206.

Golf

The FCP passes near or crosses at least eight golf courses. Indeed, Fife can justifiably claim to be the home of golf in Scotland and its leading centre. It has more than 40 courses, the basis of a multi-million pound industry that consistently attracts players and spectators from around the world to major tournaments.

St Andrews Old Course

The earliest written reference to the sport dates to 1457, when King James II banned golf and football in favour of archery. Successive Scottish kings tried to ban the game although James IV also played golf against the Earl of Bothwell in 1504. Enthusiasts also had to contend with the Kirk (Church of Scotland) which disapproved of play on Sundays. The custom lingered, and Sunday golf was banned at St Andrews until World War 2.

Golf was played at St Andrews as early as 1574. From 1735 onwards, various clubs and societies were established, including the Royal & Ancient at St Andrews in 1754, the third oldest in Scotland. Others followed at Crail, Burntisland and Kingsbarns. Of the courses themselves, the hallowed Old Course at St Andrews dates from 1764 and is still revered by golfers the world over. Courses were opened at Elie and at Kingsbarns during the 19th century.

Curiously, women's golf has its own separate history. Mary Queen of Scots is reputed to have played a version of the game in 1567, but female participation didn't really take off until the late 19th century. Interest then grew rapidly, and in Fife the first women-only club was established in 1891 at Lundin Links. However, most golf clubs restricted full membership to men, and remained men-only throughout the 20th century. By 2014 the tide of opinion had turned, and by a large majority the Royal & Ancient voted to admit women. In 2017 Muirfield followed suit and in 2018 the Royal Aberdeen was the last of the major, historic clubs to conform (with a 97% majority). By 2018, very few men-only clubs survived in Scotland, their days clearly numbered.

The British Golf Museum lies at the heart of St Andrews (opposite the Royal & Ancient Clubhouse) and houses thousands of objects including photographs, clubs and trophies. Its recent major refurbishment included a rooftop café and this fine museum is open daily: *www.britishgolfmuseum.co.uk*.

Golf professionals c. 1855: at centre Allan Robertson (regarded as the world's first professional golfer) and (second from right) Old Tom Morris, his apprentice and golf partner: see page 61

Marram grass

The Fife coast has two main types of habitat: the foreshore, and the shoreline with its inshore waters.

Spaced along the Path, several nature reserves show the vital role of the coastal margin in biodiversity and conservation. From south to north these include Torry Bay, Dumbarnie Links, Kilminning, the Eden estuary and Tentsmuir. The Isle of May, an offshore National Nature Reserve, is described on page 24.

Foreshore

The foreshore typically comprises sand dunes and grassland, rich in lime from crushed seashells. Plants are specially adapted to the harsh, salty conditions. Marram grass is common on dunes where its tough, sharp-edged leaves help to stabilise the sand, slowing coastal erosion.

Flowering plants are abundant, especially in spring. Cowslip has a cluster of deep yellow tubular flowers on a slender stem. Bloody cranesbill is a special feature at Carlingnose. Each magenta-coloured flower has several slightly notched petals on a stem growing from bushy clusters of leaves. In late summer and autumn, look out also for field gentian. It has distinctive lilac tubes from which four petals spread out.

You will probably hear the melodious, wistful song of the skylark as it soars vertically and hovers high overhead. It's small and streaky brown with white wing edges which are easier to see in flight. On the ground it forages for seeds and insects. Another common sighting, the meadow pipit looks quite similar, though more slender. Its song resembles a sequence of piping phrases ending in a trill.

Bloody cranesbill

Shoreline and inshore waters

The mudflats along the Firth of Forth and the Eden and Tay estuaries, and the salt marshes and sand banks of the Eden estuary are packed with the many tiny creatures on which numerous birds feed.

Redshank

Among them is the easily recognised curlew. It has a long curved bill and its call sounds like its name. Along the sea shores, the oystercatcher is readily identifed by its long orange bill, black head, white chest and loud piercing call. Another common species is the redshank, with its orange-red legs and noisy, yelping call. Sanderlings are less showy but are delightful to watch as they run along the edge of outgoing wavelets looking for food.

Just offshore, eider ducks often float in large flocks feeding on shellfish. The male has a black cap, white chest and back, whereas the female is mottled brown. Along the coast you may sight gannets gliding low over the water. They climb up to 30 m then fold their wings to dive-bomb their prey, reaching speeds of more than 50 mph (80 kph).

Eider duck (male)

Oystercatcher

Spotting a white-tailed sea eagle could be a highlight. Young birds were brought from Norway to a site near Balmerino and released into the wild in 2011 and 2012. With a wingspan of 8 feet (2.5 m), black wings and wedge-shaped tail, it's unmistakeable.

The Fife coast is renowned for its populations of sea mammals, although you may need patience, luck and good binoculars to spot them.

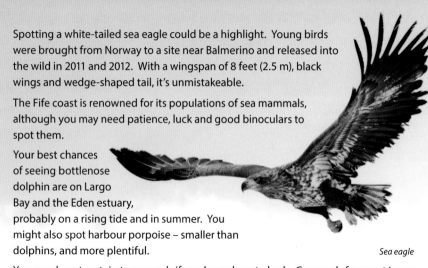

Your best chances of seeing bottlenose dolphin are on Largo Bay and the Eden estuary, probably on a rising tide and in summer. You might also spot harbour porpoise – smaller than dolphins, and more plentiful.

Sea eagle

You are almost certain to see seals if you know how to look. Grey seals frequent Largo Bay and Tentsmuir, whilst the smaller common (or harbour) seal is more prevalent in the Tay estuary – although you may see either kind anywhere on your coastal walk. Binoculars will improve the view, but are not essential. On rocky beaches, if you stare long enough at a rock you may see it arch its back and swim off!

Scotland has over a third of the world's population of grey seals, and they are more plentiful here than common seals. Telling them apart is easy if you're close enough to see the head. The grey's head is flatter, with a Roman nose, whereas the common seal has a dog-like rounded forehead and V-shaped nostrils. Greys mate between October and December, whereas common seals breed in June/July.

Grey seal

The Isle of May

Puffins on the Isle of May

Known as the 'Jewel of the Forth', this island lies about 6 miles (10 km) south-east of Anstruther, and is rich in widlife, scenery and history. Its ferry works from April to September inclusive. Because the harbour at Anstruther dries out, its departure time varies between 09.00 and 15.00, and on certain days there's no sailing. Check times and book online at www.isleofmayboattrips.co.uk.

We strongly recommend you devote an extra day to visiting The May. A typical trip lets you land and explore for about 2.5 hours. You will see and hear an amazing number of seabirds (up to 250,000) and also grey seals, over 100 of whom live and breed on The May.

Razorbill

Especially between April and July, its steep cliffs and ledges teem with seabirds such as guillemots, kittiwakes, gulls, shags, razorbills, eiders, fulmars and terns. Above all, enjoy close views of up to 100,000 puffins, which venture surprisingly close to the marked paths.

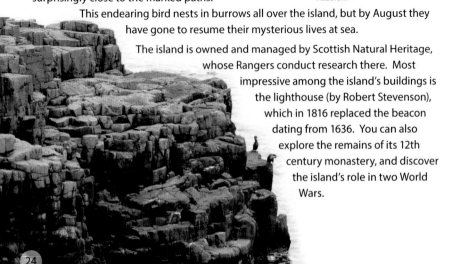

This endearing bird nests in burrows all over the island, but by August they have gone to resume their mysterious lives at sea.

The island is owned and managed by Scottish Natural Heritage, whose Rangers conduct research there. Most impressive among the island's buildings is the lighthouse (by Robert Stevenson), which in 1816 replaced the beacon dating from 1636. You can also explore the remains of its 12th century monastery, and discover the island's role in two World Wars.

3 3·1 Kincardine to North Queensferry

Distance	16·8 miles 27·0 km
Terrain	mainly tarmac, with long sections of cycleway and pavement, and a few short sections of footpath
Food and drink	Kincardine, Culross, Limekilns, Rosyth, North Queensferry
Side-trip	Culross (Palace and Gardens, Abbey)
Summary	likely to appeal more to cyclists than to walkers, this section starts with a power station and ends with heavy industry and bridges, with historic Culross as its shining highlight

Kincardine — **Culross** — **Limekilns** — **North Queensferry**

4·1 / 6·6   7·4 /11·9   5·3 / 8·5

- The route begins at Kincardine Bridge – built in 1936 and designed to swing open to allow shipping to pass upriver to Alloa. A grand archway proclaims the official start – a project managed by Fife Coast and Countryside Trust with generous support from two local businesses.

- Descend on a tarmac cycleway parallel to the A985 road, within half a mile turning right on a minor road past Inch House and Inch Farm.

- At a junction with another minor road, make a right-left dogleg and, beside the former Longannet Power Station, pick up the cycleway along the southern edge of the minor road.

- Follow the cycleway as it bends right, climbs moderately, and then undulates gently beside Longannet – in 2016 the last to close of Scotland's coal-fired power stations. Explosive demolition works took place in 2018 and decommissioning is due to complete by about 2020.

- After Longannet, the freight railway is prominent on your right. Continue on the cycleway, past various patches of woodland, to enter Torry Bay Nature Reserve with an information board at its western end. Its tidal mudflats provide overwintering for curlew, redshank, widgeon and great crested grebe; oystercatchers are common year-round.

The official start, Kincardine

- At first the path is rougher, but still easy for cyclists, then smooth again. Within 4 miles (6·4 km) of Kincardine, you pass the Culross West car park with information board. For Culross itself, turn left to divert to this amazing slice of history.

Culross

Culross is a jewel of a historic village, a tribute to nearly a century of conservation efforts by the National Trust for Scotland. Its famous buildings include the 1597 Palace with its authentic mustard-yellow render and wooden shutters (open daily in season). The Palace's walled garden is open year-round and its raised beds illustrate historic gardening techniques. They are in active use and their organic produce sells well locally.

Other highlights include the Town House (1626) and the Abbey and monastery ruins on the hillside above the village. But above all, Culross lets you enjoy its tranquil 16-17th century atmosphere as you wander around its cobbled streets and narrow wynds. And having refreshed your soul, for more tangible refreshment visit the Biscuit Café, up an alley beside the Town House. For visitor information on Culross, visit *www.nts.org.uk.*

- From the village, resume the Path past the Culross East car park, and cross the railway with care. The main Path continues to the left, but you may opt for a 2-mile detour to your right to visit Valleyfield Lagoons. They lie on a promontory of reclaimed land, formed using waste products from Longannet (ash and coal shale) with added topsoil – a wonderful environment for wading birds, insects and other wildlife.

- Beyond the lagoons, recross the railway by a high timber footbridge with long ramps. Then pass through Newmills on the pavements of the B9037.

South-east over Culross Palace

26

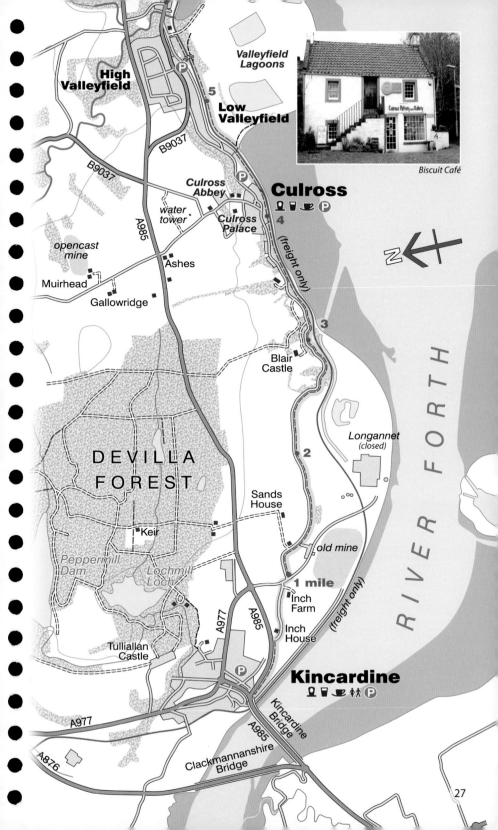

High Valleyfield

Low Valleyfield

Valleyfield Lagoons

B9037

B9037

A985

Culross Abbey

water tower

Culross Palace

Culross

Biscuit Café

5

4

(freight only)

opencast mine

Ashes

Muirhead

Gallowridge

3

Blair Castle

N

Longannet (closed)

DEVILLA FOREST

Sands House

2

Keir

Peppermill Dam

Lochmill Loch

old mine

1 mile

Inch Farm

Tulliallan Castle

A977

A985

Inch House

(freight only)

R I V E R   F O R T H

Kincardine

A977

A985

Kincardine Bridge

A876

Clackmannanshire Bridge

- Just after you enter Torryburn under a railway bridge, look for a traffic island where the path turns right down towards the shore of Torry Bay.

- After 600 m, the Path turns left to zigzag steeply uphill beside a fine old stone wall. At the top of this climb, turn right along a farm road between fields.

- After 0·5 mile (800 m), the farm road meets a minor road where you bear left to join it. Follow the minor road until it reaches the busy A985, where you pick up a roadside cycleway – mercifully briefly.

- Within 300 m, escape the heavy traffic at Crombie by turning right into Farm Road, which bends left to become Orchard Grove then Little Foothorn. This last street narrows to a footpath, then, sadly, it rejoins the A985.

- Although you are on a reserved cycleway, it adjoins the main road for a full mile, and you will feel buffeting and noise from fast-moving oncoming traffic.

- Turn right (signed for Charlestown and Limekilns) on a rough road that makes a left/ right dogleg past the Scottish Lime Centre: see page 17. Descend to Charlestown, where walkers use the pavement and cyclists the road, and continue into Limekilns with good views of the Forth bridges ahead.

- In Limekilns, turn right off the Promenade and pass through Bruce Haven, at first on a road, then on a cycleway. Ignore a tempting fingerpost pointing left up an old coffin road and instead keep to the shoreside cycleway.

- You reach the ruins of Rosyth Old Church with its interesting graveyard. Shortly afterwards, the Path veers left up a long, steep hill, with views over the giant crane and dry docks of Rosyth to your right.

- Descend to the busy A895 roadside cycleway again, to endure a further mile of heavy traffic presence. The FCP signage ignores the cycleway sign pointing right down Hilton Road, and instead sticks with the A895 roadside cycleway/pavement until just before a large roundabout.

- Turn right to follow the tarmac footpath southward, soon picking up a road (Wilson Way) that you follow around to the right until it reaches Hilton Road at a T-junction. (This is where you rejoin the cycle route which turned off the A895 earlier.)

Rosyth Old Church

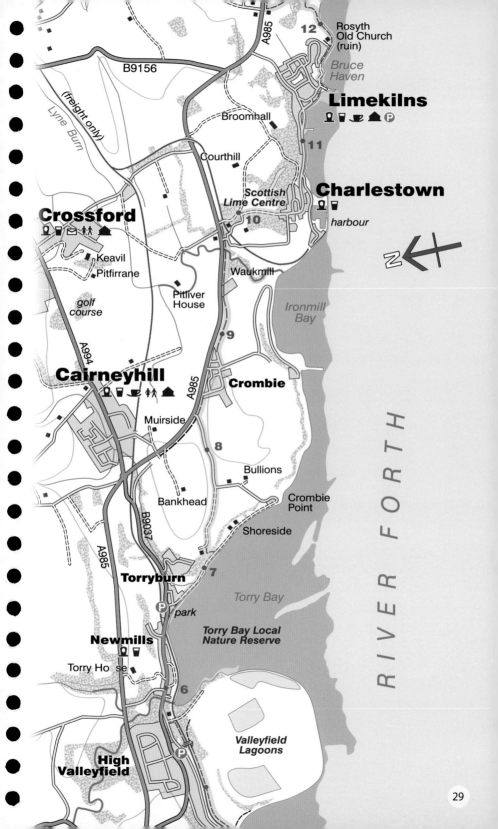

B9156

(freight only)

Lyne Burn

A985

12 Rosyth
Old Church
(ruin)

*Bruce
Haven*

Limekilns

♟ 🍺 🛶 ⛺ 🅿

11

Broomhall

Courthill

*Scottish
Lime Centre*

Charlestown
♟ 🍺

harbour

Crossford
♟ 🍺 ✉ 🚹🚺 ⛺

Keavil

Pitfirrane

Pitliver
House

*golf
course*

Waukmill

10

*Ironmill
Bay*

9

N

Cairneyhill
♟ 🍺 🛶 🚹🚺 ⛺

A994

A985

Muirside

Crombie

8

Bullions

Bankhead

B9037

Crombie
Point

Shoreside

A985

R I V E R   F O R T H

Torryburn

🅿 *park*

7

Torry Bay

Newmills
♟ 🍺

Torry House

6

*Torry Bay Local
Nature Reserve*

High
Valleyfield

🅿

*Valleyfield
Lagoons*

29

- Turn left (eastward) along Hilton Road, using the pedestrian crossing to reach its south side. Within 300 m you approach another roundabout and need to cross another busy main road (Castle Road) to continue south-east on the relative safety of Ferry Toll Road.
- On your right is Rosyth Europarc, a business park fringed by a wavy blue fence. Near its end, turn right through its gates and go down past its car park. Turn left at the fingerpost (signed 'Heritage Trail') on a path that descends past a 16th century dovecote with information board.
- The path emerges at Milne Road: look ahead for the ruined Rosyth Castle, a tower house which dates from the 1470s. Its impact is marred by the surrounding high fence and naval industry, a sad contrast with its former splendid isolation, almost cut off by the Forth. For a closer look, cross the road and detour right for 100 m to enter Rosyth dockyard, then cross the railway to reach the castle within a further 100 m.
- Otherwise, at Milne Road turn left and follow broad pavements, keeping straight over a roundabout to reach a crossroads after 0·7 miles (1·1 km). Turn right at the traffic lights to follow the B981 for North Queensferry.

Queensferry Crossing from the B981

- The view ahead is dominated by the Forth and its bridges. The B981 snakes its way towards the gleaming Queensferry Crossing, passing beneath its approach road. After the underpass, the B981 continues past a hotel and descends to the older bridge within 650 m.
- The B891 goes on into North Queensferry, morphing into its Main Street to reach the magnificent giant steel Forth Bridge just 800 m beyond the road bridge.
- To divert to the station at North Queensferry, note that it is about 150 feet above you! The only access is by a stiff climb up The Brae, so turn left off Main Street before passing under the railway bridge.

i **Three Forth bridges**

The Path passes beneath three spectacular bridges in close succession. From west to east, they are the 2017 Queensferry Crossing, the 1964 Forth road bridge and the original Forth Bridge which carries the mainline railway. Opened in 1890, this cantilever structure was the world's first giant steel bridge. It has become a national icon and landmark, and in 2015 was inscribed as Scotland's sixth World Heritage Site.

The original suspension road bridge had become overloaded with traffic, and 50 years later a new cable-stayed road bridge was commissioned. Most vehicles use the M90 over the new bridge, whilst public transport, bikes and mopeds use the older bridge: see **www.forth-bridges.co.uk**.

3·2 North Queensferry to Burntisland

Distance	11·8 miles 19·0 km
Terrain	mainly footpath with some pavement and little tarmac; mostly flat with some flights of steps
Food and drink	North Queensferry, Inverkeithing, Dalgety Bay, Aberdour, Burntisland
Side-trip	Aberdour Castle and Gardens, St Fillan's Church (adjacent)
Summary	a varied section with quarries, beaches and bays, patches of woodland and good wildlife on the water; a worthy prelude to Fife's coastal attractions

North Queensferry ──── 4·7/7·6 ──── **Dalgety Bay** ──── 3·5/5·6 ──── **Aberdour** ──── 3·6/5·8 ──── **Burntisland**

- If arriving by train, exit North Queensferry station and descend steeply down the road (The Brae) until you pick up the FCP signage.

- Turn left at the foot where an FCP fingerpost stands beside the Napoleon Well. This was the original start of the route before its extension to Kincardine. Local schoolchildren celebrated the opening by making collages that are set into the wall.

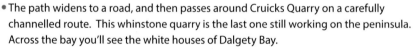

- The rocky path descends beneath the stone pillar of the Forth Bridge to enter Carlingnose Point Wildlife Reserve. On your left, a modern house perches dramatically on the cliff above the disused quarry. Ahead and to the right, the ruined pier is an important nesting site for terns.

- The path widens to a road, and then passes around Cruicks Quarry on a carefully channelled route. This whinstone quarry is the last one still working on the peninsula. Across the bay you'll see the white houses of Dalgety Bay.

- You return almost to the line of the railway before turning right along Hope Street into the Royal Burgh of Inverkeithing. Beside the modern Civic Centre there's an information board showing its historic buildings, notably the Mercat Cross and Parish Church. It's worth a minor detour to explore Inverkeithing's historic centre.

- To resume the Path, turn right down Townhall Street, then right into Commercial Road. Opposite the railway footbridge, turn left along Preston Crescent. Follow the crescent as it swings left, leaving a large tract of green reclaimed land on your right.

- Head for the Stone Marine building and pass along to its left to reach a broad tarmac path, resembling a road with its streetlamps.

Two of the bridges from North Queensferry

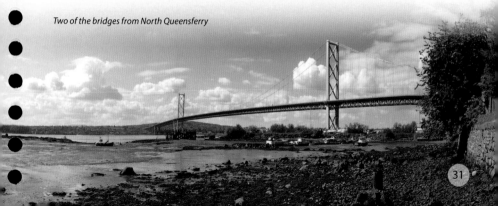

- Soon there is woodland to your left, with plenty of seabird life on the waters of St David's Harbour. The tarmac cycleway goes nearly to the headland, then a short stony path leads up to pavement, more path and more pavement.

- The route now turns right down a narrow path that descends by steps; cyclists keep straight on. This charming path rounds the headland, passing through woods before rising briefly to rejoin the suburban road with its large brick houses. There are some good views across to Inchcolm and its abbey: see the panel on page 35.

- A longer stretch of wooded path goes beside Dalgety Bay with its eider ducks, woodpeckers and other bird life. This section culminates with the superb ruins of St Bridget's Kirk, with an information board.

- Turn left on a road uphill briefly, then right along a road lined with beech trees, and in spring with daffodils. Pass a communications mast on the left, then look for a right turn downhill and through an underpass.

- For 0·7 mile (1·1 km) from St Colme House to Aberdour, the Path follows the golf club road. Where it ends, continue ahead on the public road and turn right into Aberdour, an attractive village which grew up around its harbour and prospered further after the arrival of the railway in 1890.

- Within 150 m, the Path turns right down Shore Road, but it's worth keeping straight on briefly to the 1910 memorial clock. Follow the signs ahead to visit Aberdour Castle and Gardens and its 12th century neighbour, St Fillan's Church: see panel.

- Resume the Path to descend Shore Road and turn left beside the beach. A fine 'Prospect from Aberdour' information board on the promenade identifies the wonderful view from here: north is at the foot of its map.

> **ℹ Aberdour Castle**
>
> Begun in the 12th century as a stone tower house, the castle buildings evolved over the next 500 years as successive owners extended it eastward to suit their needs. In the 16th century, James Douglas, Earl of Morton added the central range and terraced gardens, with an impressive stone dovecot. A century later, the 7th Earl of Morton added the east range to create better living quarters for his family. After a serious fire, only partial repairs were made, and in 1725 the family abandoned the castle. It is now cared for by Historic Environment Scotland: **www.historicenvironment.scot**. Adjacent to the castle, don't miss St Fillan's, the 12th-century Norman church which has been beautifully restored.

Aberdour Castle

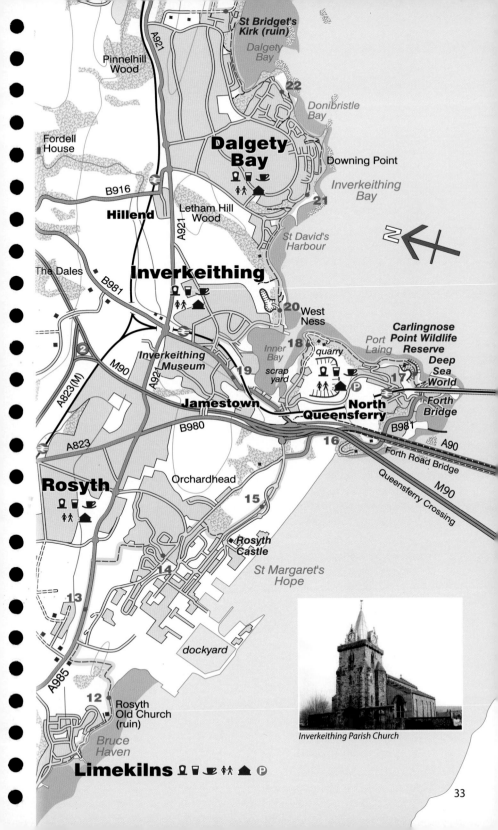

St Bridget's Kirk (ruin)

Dalgety Bay

Pinnelhill Wood

A921

22

Donibristle Bay

Fordell House

Dalgety Bay

Downing Point

B916

Inverkeithing Bay

21

Hillend

Letham Hill Wood

A921

St David's Harbour

The Dales

B981

Inverkeithing

N

20 West Ness

Carlingnose Point Wildlife Reserve

Port Laing

18 *quarry*

2

M90

A823(M)

A921

Inverkeithing Museum

Inner Bay

19 *scrap yard*

Deep Sea World

17

Jamestown

B980

P

North Queensferry

Forth Bridge

A823

16

B981

A90

Forth Road Bridge

Rosyth

Orchardhead

15

Queensferry Crossing

M90

◆ **Rosyth Castle**

14

St Margaret's Hope

13

dockyard

A985

12 Rosyth Old Church (ruin)

Bruce Haven

Limekilns

Inverkeithing Parish Church

33

- Bear left uphill at the boat club, and follow the undulating path that leads around the craggy headland.
- The path narrows as it approaches fences in front of Hawkcraig cottage, but don't pass the cottage: instead look behind you for a steep flight of stone steps.
- Climb the steps and follow the Path as it descends more gently to the Admiralty research station that was crucial in the World War 2 fight against U-boats. Few clear remnants remain, but there are great views from this headland.
- Turn left along the road and pass Silversands beach (with warnings of its soft sinking sands). The path – sometimes tarmac, sometimes softer – undulates beside the rocky shore. The walk is punctuated by trains passing along the line, nearby on the left.
- Turn left to pass under the railway though a fine stone tunnel, then climb the ramp beyond and continue ahead until you reach the Starley Burn falls. After the falls, the path is constrained between stone walls and timber fence, running between private grounds and the railway.
- About 2 miles (3 km) after Silversands, houses start to appear, and you're arriving at Burntisland. The path broadens and the grassy slope to its left gradually morphs into a recreation space.
- You reach a crossroads with Kirkton Road: turn right. The road climbs, then descends to a T-junction. Turn left along the High Street, passing some handsome Victorian buildings near the centre of Burntisland.

Starley Burn falls

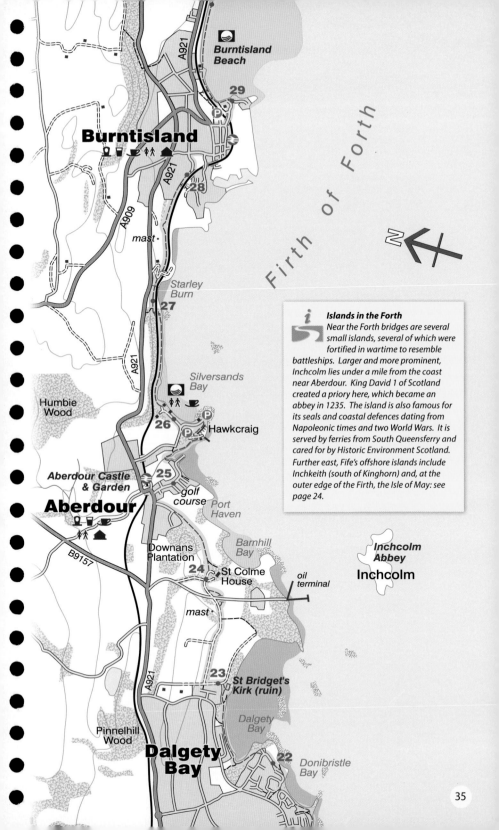

A921

Burntisland Beach

29

P

Burntisland

A921

28

Firth of Forth

N

A909

mast ·

A921

Starley Burn

27

Silversands Bay

26

P

P

Hawkcraig

A921

Humbie Wood

Aberdour Castle & Garden

25

golf course

Aberdour

Port Haven

B9157

Barnhill Bay

Downans Plantation

24 St Colme House

oil terminal

mast ·

Inchcolm Abbey

Inchcolm

23 **St Bridget's Kirk (ruin)**

Dalgety Bay

Pinnelhill Wood

A921

Dalgety Bay

22 *Donibristle Bay*

---

i **Islands in the Forth**
Near the Forth bridges are several small islands, several of which were fortified in wartime to resemble battleships. Larger and more prominent, Inchcolm lies under a mile from the coast near Aberdour. King David 1 of Scotland created a priory here, which became an abbey in 1235. The island is also famous for its seals and coastal defences dating from Napoleonic times and two World Wars. It is served by ferries from South Queensferry and cared for by Historic Environment Scotland. Further east, Fife's offshore islands include Inchkeith (south of Kinghorn) and, at the outer edge of the Firth, the Isle of May: see page 24.

3·3 Burntisland to Leven

Distance	16·5 miles 26·6 km
Terrain	after glorious beach walking, there's lots of tarmac through Kirkcaldy, then woodland and shoreside path (with flights of steps) ending with unrelieved urban tarmac
Food and drink	Burntisland, Kirkcaldy, Dysart, West Wemyss, Buckhaven, Methil, Leven
Side-trips	Ravenscraig Castle, Fife Coastal Centre (Dysart), Wemyss Caves
Summary	interesting walking with fine castles, beaches, harbours and amazing cave carvings; the final 3 miles may be better completed on a bus

Burntisland ——— **Kirkcaldy** ——— **Wemyss Caves** ——— **Leven**

5·9/9·5   6·5 /10·5   4·1/6·6

- Follow the High Street to its eastern end. Turn right down Links Place, then left along Lammerlaws Road.

- The road crosses the railway to reach a roundabout. Go straight over, past the Beacon Leisure Centre, and, keeping it on your left, reach the promenade. At its end, exit through two sets of pillars.

- Here, an FCP fingerpost points to a choice: turn right for the main route across the beach, or left for the high-tide route beside the main road (or for accommodation along the Kinghorn Road). If you aren't sure about the tide, carefully study the information board at the start of the beach.

- The main Path follows Burntisland Beach and Pettycur Bay, passing the two escape routes on the left, and ascending a sandy ramp near its end. At the top, an information board and fingerpost point out the main route along Pettycur Road, with a high tide alternative inland.

- After Pettycur Road rounds the headland, look for the lamp-post with a sign pointing right down Doo-dells Lane to a curved metal bench and information board.

- Follow the black metal railings down a zigzag path to the sandy beach of Kinghorn Harbour, with views to Inchkeith offshore.

- Pass the lifeboat station and boat club and turn left at the end, up Nethergate.

- Go under the railway arch to the fingerpost that sends you right through the park on a paved path.

- Turn right under the railway, then left beside it on a path channelled between the caravan park and railway. As it descends, views open out along the rocky shoreline. The path undulates, then climbs towards the railway. Later it reaches the splendid ruins of Seafield Tower, the remains of a castle built in the 16th century from local red sandstone.

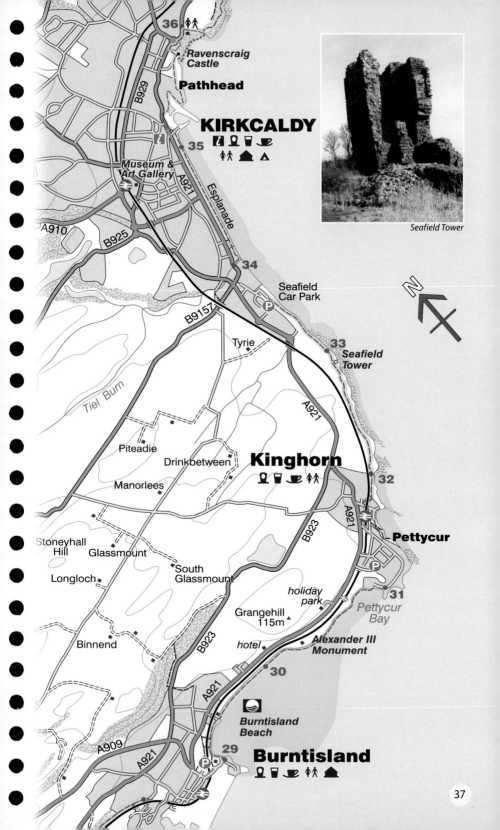

Ravenscraig
Castle

Pathhead

KIRKCALDY

35

Museum &
Art Gallery

A910

B925

34

Seafield
Car Park

P

Tyrie

33 **Seafield
Tower**

Seafield Tower

B9157

A921

Tiel Burn

Piteadie

Drinkbetween

Kinghorn

Manorlees

32

Stoneyhall
Hill   Glassmount

Longloch

South
Glassmount

A921

B923

Pettycur

P

holiday
park

31

Pettycur
Bay

Grangehill
115m

Binnend

B923

hotel

**Alexander III
Monument**

A921

30

Burntisland
Beach

A909

A921

29

P

Burntisland

- Pass through a kissing-gate onto a broad stony path: the houses on the left are on the outskirts of Kirkcaldy. The town was birthplace of Adam Smith (1723-90), the father of modern economics. It was also a world centre for producing linoleum: see page 19. Its nickname 'the lang toun' (long town) derives from its long main street.
- Pass the ruins of a pier and cross Seafield Park. At the end of the park, turn left then right along Seafield Road. At the fuel station, turn right down the Esplanade and follow it as it bends towards the shore.
- The Esplanade has been refurbished as a die-straight motorway of broad tarmac lined with walls of white concrete. Mercifully, after 1·2 miles the Esplanade finally ends, and you bear right past Babyland to follow the main road eastward, ignoring cycleway signs that point uphill.
- Follow the busy High Street uphill for 350 m to the main entrance of Carr's Hutchisons Mill. Turn right into the site, watching out for lorries.

- Follow signs through the flour mill, and turn right at the waste water treatment plant. The factory noise soon recedes as you pick up a loose-surfaced path that meanders towards Pathhead Sands, an attractive reclaimed grassy space with sandy beach.
- Ravenscraig Castle stands before you on its headland; the tarmac path crosses an access road and veers right to a choice point just beneath the castle, with fingerpost and map.

Ravenscraig Castle from the shore

- Here the route divides: the high tide option climbs a flight of steps to the A921 where you bear right across a roundabout into Dysart Road and enter Ravenscraig Park. (From here a 200-metre detour to the right would take you inside the wonderful ruins of Ravenscraig Castle.) Follow signs through the park down to the shoreline, through mature woodland with massive crags and serpentine stone walls, to rejoin the low tide option after 550 m.

- The low-tide option follows a hand-railed path around the rocky headland, past Castle Cave and around a shingle beach. Near its end, climb the 40-step stone staircase to pass the Ravenscraig Doocot and rejoin the high-tide route.

Shingle beach with stone staircase

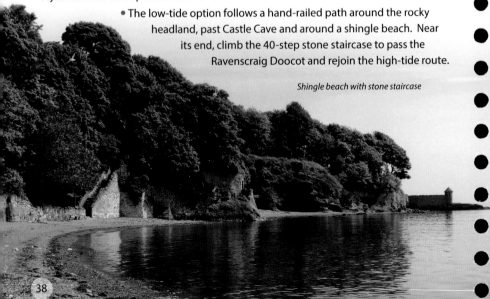

- At the shoreline, the joint route leaves the park at a small headland and continues on a shoreside path. Pass through the dramatic Harbour Tunnel through bare rock to emerge at Dysart's fine harbour.

- On your left is the 18th-century stone Harbourmaster's House, home to the Fife Coast and Countryside Trust. The Harbour Bistro is on the ground floor (open daily year-round) and the Coastal Centre houses interesting displays about Fife's coastal geology, fossils and wildlife in the basement.

- After the Harbourmaster's House, continue beside the shore along the Pan Ha' and turn left steeply up Hie-Gait and climb the concrete steps. At the top, turn right along Howard Place.

- Bear left up The Walk, then turn right along High Street, which goes uphill (Edington Place) and continues as a path parallel to the shore. Within 300 m, pass the memorial and winding gear of Frances Colliery, reminders of Fife's mining heritage: see page 17.

- Leaving behind the industrial relics, the path soon descends by a flight of stone steps to a pebbly beach. Follow a lovely informal path set back from the shore, surrounded by trees and alive with birdsong.

- Approaching West Wemyss, pass the ruins of a building and a disused quarry, worth a detour to look at the sandstone rockface. The path ends at a car park.

- Cross to Buckhaven & Wemyss Parish Church (also known as St Adrian's), then continue between the church and grassy area. On the left, Castle Wemyss (privately owned) perches above you on the clifftop.

West Wemyss rockface

- A notice asks you to walk along the beach, rather than the path, for 500 m. Pass through a gap in the wall on the left and continue beside the shore.

- The path becomes a road beside fenced-off Coal Authority land, with a warning of unstable ground from the former Michael Colliery. At a fingerpost, fork left inland a bit on a path that's grassy at first, then muddy or stony, to divert around the back of a large scrap yard protected by razor and barbed wire.

- Return to the sea wall for the next section. You can't fail to notice Buckhaven's huge turbine ahead, and across the water, you may pick out the conical shape of North Berwick Law to your right.

- Just after a memorial to Jimmy Shand, a former miner turned famous accordionist, the information board alerts you to Wemyss Caves, very soon on the left. They are home to an amazing range of Pictish, Viking and Christian carvings: see ***www.wemysscaves.org***.

- Climb a longish flight of gravel-filled timber steps (with an informal bike ramp beside it) to reach the ruins of the Macduff Castle.
- Continue between the castle wall and a fence, and turn left at a field edge. Then (just before reaching the main road) turn right along a farm road that follows a former railway.

- The trackbed is pleasantly embanked between fields and partly tree-lined. After some steps, continue to head for Buckhaven's turbine. Where the path ends, turn right at a hoarding and descend a few steps to the road (Viewforth).
- Follow Viewforth as it bends left and becomes Randolph Street, then College Street (with bus stop), a gloomy section. It ends at a roundabout where you bear right into Wellesley Road.
- Pass an information board that explains how trams used to run down this wide street. Continue along the road, passing car sales yards and, eventually, an information board about renewable energy in Fife beside the derelict Methil dock area.

Macduff Castle

- You follow Wellesley Road for about 0·7 miles (1·1 km) passing the Randolph Wemyss Memorial Hospital en route. At the junction with a dual carriageway (Sea Road), bear right down the High Street.
- Bear slightly left at a roundabout to stay on the High Street, passing blocks of flats and houses, and follow it in a left-right dogleg. Eventually you reach Methil Heritage Centre, open on certains afternoons, admission free: www.methilheritage.org.uk.
- After what feels like miles of High Street but is actually only 1·5 miles (2·5 km), it finally reaches South Street where you turn left.
- This rises to a roundabout beside the River Leven, where you turn right to cross by the Bawbee Bridge. Cross the river and keep to the main road (A955) past Levenmouth Swimming Pool, finally escaping the traffic and urban environment only at its beach.
- If after reading this route description you decide to save your energy for pleasanter walking, you can take a bus from College Street, Buckhaven to Leven Bus Station (opposite Levenmouth Swimming Pool). Buses are frequent during daylight hours (about six per hour except Sundays) and you can thus avoid 3 miles (4·8 km) of unrelieved tarmac and urban decay.

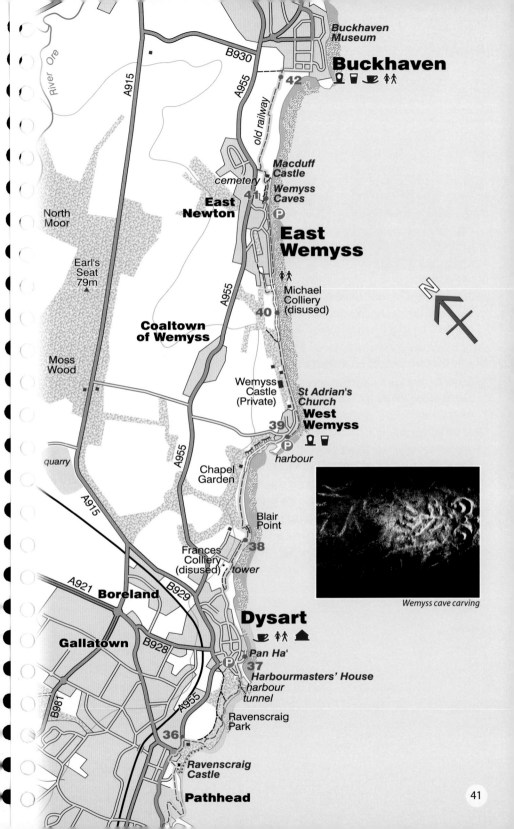

Wemyss cave carving

- Pass through a kissing-gate and follow the trackbed for about 0·7 mile (1·1 km). At its end, descend steps to cross into Dumbarnie Links Wildlife Reserve (SWT): see information board. Again, there's a choice of routes, with the beach being available at most states of the tide and a route above the dunes for high tide.

- Notice two concrete pillboxes dating from World War 2, one of which is sealed off and acts as a bat colony. An information board explains how SWT is combatting dune 'blow-out' using arrays of chestnut paling fence to stabilise the marram grass.

- Near the end of the beach, a fingerpost confirms where the low-tide route ends in order to follow an inland route that uses two timber footbridges to cross the Cocklemill Burn.

- Pass through the gap in a row of pine trees and head straight over for Shell Bay Caravan Park. Continue past static and touring caravans to a junction where there's an information board, perhaps with a nearby pile of crushed shells.

- Go right, then left across a footbridge and up a winding, undulating path with super views over Shell Bay.

- Kincraig Point is the eastern end of Shell Bay, and the western end of the Chainwalk (far below you): see page 46. After you round the corner, the Chainwalk path rises steeply to join the FCP about 100 m beyond the benches.

- Continue along the clifftop walk with its look-out posts and gun emplacement, communications mast, plentiful wildflowers and great views all round.

- The narrow path descends to the dunes and a fingerpost points out the onward tidal routes: low-tide across the beach of West Bay, or high-tide beside the golf course (Earlsferry Links). The unmarked path heading west from here along the shore gives east-to-west access to the Chainwalk.

- At the end of West Bay, the beach route climbs to rejoin the golf course route. Cross the Links (with care) on a well-marked track, then turn right to follow a grassy path leading to Chapel Green Road, which soon becomes Earlsferry High Street.

- Keep straight on to reach the centre of Elie within half a mile (800 m). Elie Parish Church stands at the corner of the A917 main road. Just before Toll Green, with its bus shelter and historic photographs, Elie High Street broadens out.

Shell Bay, near Kincraig Point

Abercrombie

Newark Farm

Bowhouse

Newark Castle (ruin)

B917

B942

57 miles

Ardross Castle (ruin)

Ardross Farm

A917

Sauchar Point

Balbuthie

Kilconquhar Castle Estate and Country Club

Kilconquhar Loch

Elie House

56

Shepherd's Knowe ℗

Lady's Tower

Ruby Bay

Wood Haven lighthouse

55

B942

B941

Kilconquhar

A917

Elie

Elie Harbour

Cairnie House

B941

St. Ford

Chapel Ness *ruin*

54

Colinsburgh

Earlsferry

golf course

Muircambus

West Bay

B942

A917

53

St. Ford Links ℗

masts

Dunotter

Cocklemill Burn

Kincraig

Shell Bay Caravan Park

ruin

N

A917

old railway

Dumbarnie Links Wildlife Reserve

51

Shell Bay

52

Kincraig Point

Ruddons Point

50

Drumeldrie

ruins

Largo Bay

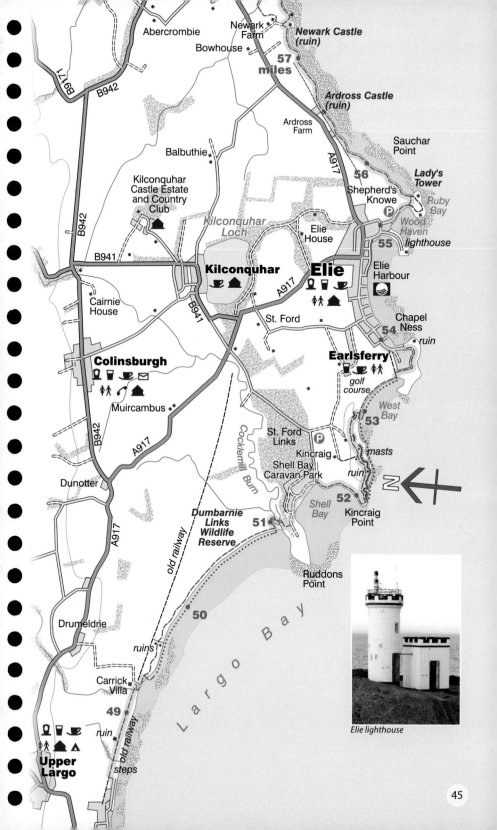

Elie lighthouse

Carrick Villa

old railway

49

ruin

old railway

Upper Largo

steps

45

The Elie Chainwalk

For some, this challenging option is the highlight of their holiday, whilst others won't be tempted for a second. It's a scrambling route of about 500 m across rocky beaches with caves, cliffs and volcanic rock formations, with eight steel chains providing handholds for the most difficult sections. Scotland's secret via ferrata offers a unique way to experience the rocky coastline around Kincraig Point (just west of Earlsferry Links). The Chainwalk is thought to have been created by locals in about 1920. Nowadays it is maintained by Fife Council, which last replaced most of the chains in 2010.

Official warning notices at each end explain that the scramble is hazardous, that some chains have vertical height gain/loss of up to 10 metres, and that you should allow 1-3 hours. Some of the rocky ascents and descents have awkward footholds, and you need upper body strength to cling on where the rock overhangs (e.g. the easternmost chain). It demands a degree of agility and stamina, and is unsuitable for anybody with restricted mobility or a fear of heights. If in doubt about a member of your group, have a fallback plan. Please read to the end before deciding whether to commit yourself: there are no escape routes.

We provide links to detailed descriptions at *www.rucsacs.com/links/fcp*.

Reduce the risk of injury, and of needlessly calling out the emergency services, as follows:

- **Don't go alone, especially in winter.**
- **Plan your departure time based on the state of the tide: see page 47.**
- **Approach the route from east to west.**
- **Wear suitable footwear with well-gripping soles; consider taking gloves.**

It's vital to know both the timing and the height of high tide and plan accordingly: see page 13. There are several constraints:

The first chain can't be reached until an hour or two after high tide; after a really high tide you may have to wait longer if the access is still awash or the rock too wet and slippery.

You won't know how long it will take you to complete unless you have done it before.

The route is easier around low tide, so if possible set off some time from three hours before low tide up to an hour or so after it. Avoid setting out on a rising tide unless you are certain of having ample time plus a safety margin.

Assuming you are walking the main Path west-east as recommended, doing the Chainwalk east-west involves doubling back. Unless you are experienced, we think it is prudent to start with the easternmost chain – the most challenging, so best tackled while you are fresh. If this chain is too difficult, it's better to find that out straight away. Later chains are less daunting when heading west. Also, the eastern end of the Chainwalk is easier to locate, beginning at a path marked by an FCP fingerpost: see page 44 bullet 6. If staying overnight in Elie, seize the chance to ditch your rucksack, or at least to lose most of its weight: a large rucksack will give extra trouble on certain chains.

So, is it worth it? Our account is based on two attempts, the first unsuccessful, the second an enjoyable completion. An obvious reward is the physical sense of achievement from a rocky scramble above breaking waves. A further payoff is the insights into coastal geology that you gain from the towering columns of basalt, the sea caves and natural arches and the volcanic rocks on a wave-cut platform. The risks are obvious from the outset: please take the above advice seriously. Each person must assess the risks and rewards for themselves.

Facing page:
upper– First chain at low tide
lower– Columns of basalt tower over walker

This page:
upper– First chain at mid tide
lower– A 10-metre descent chain

3·5 Elie to Crail

Distance	**11.0 miles 17·7 km**
Terrain	mostly flattish mixture of pavements, coastal and other paths, rocky stretches, ending on pavement
Food and drink	Elie, St Monans, Pittenweem, Anstruther, Crail
Side trips	Anstruther Fisheries Museum, Crail Museum & Heritage Centre
Summary	excellent shoreside and cliff-edge walking interspersed with superbly maintained buildings in old fishing villages; wide views frame historic sites and an unusual natural feature

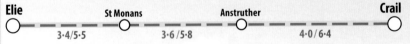

Elie   **St Monans**   **Anstruther**   **Crail**

3·4/5·5   3·6/5·8   4·0/6·4

- From Toll Green, turn right along Stenton Row down to the shore. Turn left along Admiralty Lane, then right along a lane to the shore.

- From a parking area, follow a signposted path through grassy dunes. After about 150 m the official route turns left, but it's worth making a small diversion along a clear path ahead. It approaches the distinctive lighthouse and passes Lady's Tower, then goes above Ruby Bay to rejoin the main route.

Elie Parish Church

Romantic ruins of Lady's Tower

Caiplie

63

West
Pitcorthie

Cornceres

Cuttyskelly

Blacklaws

caravan
park

P

Cellardyke
harbour

B9171

Kilrenny

A917

62

**Anstruther
Easter**

B9131

Scottish
Fisheries
Museum

Anstruther

🛈 👤 🍺 ☕ 👫 🏛

🛈

P

harbour

61

**Anstruther
Wester**

Billow
Ness

Easter
Grangemuir

60

Grangemuir
House

St Fillan's
Cave

Pittenweem

👤 🍺 ☕ 👫 🏕

Break
Boats

B942

P
👫

Blind
Capul

59

A917

St Monans
Windmill

saltpans

P

58

St Monans

👤 🍺 ☕ 👫 🏕 ⛺

Craigiewells

Partan
Craig

Newark
Farm

**St Monans
Church**
tower

Bowhouse

**Newark Castle
(ruin)**

57

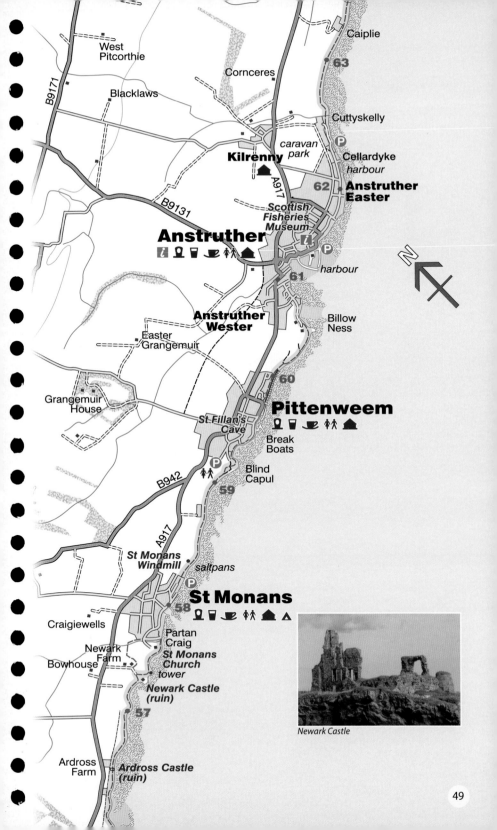

Newark Castle

Ardross
Farm

**Ardross Castle
(ruin)**

N

- With excellent views south and east to North Berwick Law, Bass Rock and Isle of May, a path above the shore leads to Ardross Farm and Castle. You can access a farm shop and the main road here via a track below the old railway trackbed: see page 68. The path goes between the two surviving sections of the castle, dating from the mid-14th to 16th centuries.

- Continue along the undulating path, with some steps. Below Newark Castle, note warnings about dogs, grazing cattle and high tide.

- Go up and through a gate. Shortly the alternative route leads left through another gate. Further on, bear right and follow a field-edge path. At a junction, turn right and continue to a minor road and on to rejoin the main Path near the church.

- On the main route, you pass a 16th century dovecote as you approach Newark Castle. Its western part fell into the sea long ago, but most of its ground floor is still visible, if unstable. Take care if you inspect these ruins!

- The path continues just above the shore and passes below St Monans Church. Climb narrow steps in its stone-built sea defence to reach the church entrance: see panel.

- Follow a signposted tarmac path between cottages to a minor road. Keep right, down West End to St Monans harbour.

---

i **St Monans Church**
Built as a chapel in the 1360s, this sandstone church is the closest to the sea in Scotland, only 20 m from the cliff edge. Its name may come from 'Monance', a little known saint.

It became the local parish church in 1646. Its unusual shape, a truncated cross, is topped by an octagonal tower. The church is roofed with Cumberland slate. Inside it is pleasantly light, thanks to the extensive use of limewash (paint) on almost every surface. Visitors are welcome daily, from April to October: see www.scottishchurches.org.uk.

Old Pittenweem on the waterfront

- At a junction on the left, continue ahead along Mid Shore. To borrow a key for the windmill, turn left along Station Road and left into West Street for 50 m to the Spar shop; return afterwards to Mid Shore.

- On the main route, at a four-way junction, bear left up to Rose Street and turn right, past fine stone terrace houses to a car park and wide path above the shore.

- Approaching St Monans Windmill, note the tidal swimming pool, although at high tide it's submerged. The best view of the nearby salt pans is from the windmill itself.

- At the east end of the site an information panel explains the surviving stonework of a panhouse here. Follow the wide path ahead.

- After a few hundred metres, it forks: follow the path to the left, up steps to a park. Pass a shelter to a path above the shore, and go on to a small park on the edge of Pittenweem.

- The path leads between houses and the sea wall to a road. Veer right to the esplanade, and continue past the harbour, crowded with fishing boats. The harbour was improved by Sir John Anstruther (1718-1799) in conjunction with his enterprise at St Monans. He was also the local MP on three occasions.

- Continue along Mid Shore. To reach the town centre bear left up Water Wynd. Otherwise, follow East Shore past beautiful stone buildings. At the far end of the harbour go left up Abbey Wall Road on the east side. At a bend, go through a gap in the wall along a cobbled path.

- Cross a small park and follow a path for about 200 m. Bear right down to the edge of a golf course

 St Monans Windmill

This, the sole surviving windmill in Fife, was built in the late 18th century by Sir John Anstruther whose Newark Coal & Salt Company opened a mine nearby. Nine salt pans (still visible) were dug on the beach below and roofed over. The windmill pumped sea water to the pans where coal was burned to evaporate the water. The salt residue was sent by rail to Pittenweem harbour, and used mainly in food preservation. Salt production ceased around 1820. To visit the windmill, borrow a key from the Spar shop which is open until 9 pm and means a round trip detour of about 2 km.

- White stakes mark the golf curse boundary, and the Path. At a fork go straight on, soon past a tiny shell beach. Then, encouragingly, Anstruther comes into view.

- Cross a small park to a wide tarmac path above the beach and go on to a minor road, soon passing Anstruther Golf Club (1890). After about 50 m turn right along Shore Road to a T-junction; turn left into the narrow, busy High Street.

- Follow it to a roundabout and turn right, down to the sea front. Go past the marina and harbour – boats leave here for the Isle of May (page 24), and the Fisheries Museum is opposite (page 18).

At Cellardyke harbour

- Continue on the path beside James Street, with a building proclaiming its date as 1723.

- At Tolbooth Wynd, cross diagonally right to John Street, with terraced houses of various sizes and architectural styles. After about 700 m you reach Cellardyke harbour, with its narrow entrance.

- Continue for another 250 m past a park on left, then go straight on to a car park. At Kilrenny Mill Caravan Park, tarmac yields to a vehicle track, then a shoreside path.

- About 700 m further on, pass Caiplie houses. After another 500 m, cross a stone wall on a step stile. Continue to the unusual low, tiered sandstone outcrop that is Caiplie Caves. Early Christian crosses are carved on the wall of the largest cave, but explore with care as rock falls aren't unknown.

- A grassy path leads on and in another 500 m, as you cross a stone wall, note the warning about dogs and livestock. Then follow about 200 m of rocky going and a path across a low headland.

- With the harbour in view, go up to the main road in Crail and right to Shoregate in the town centre

- Crail Museum & Heritage Centre is worth a visit. It features displays about its church, golf, farming, fishing and the port, and both World Wars. For opening times, visit *www.crailmuseum.org.uk*.

Caiplie Caves

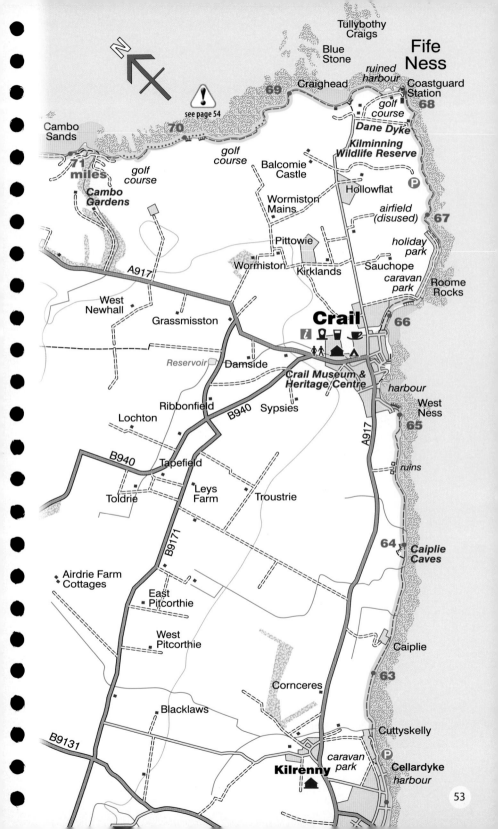

N

see page 54

Tullybothy Craigs

Blue Stone

Fife Ness

ruined harbour

Craighead

69

Coastguard Station

68

golf course

Dane Dyke

Cambo Sands

70

Kilminning Wildlife Reserve

71 miles

golf course

golf course

Balcomie Castle

Hollowflat

P

Cambo Gardens

golf course

Wormiston Mains

airfield (disused)

67

Pittowie

holiday park

A917

Wormiston

Kirklands

Sauchope

caravan park

Roome Rocks

West Newhall

Grassmisston

Crail

i *♀* *♂* *♨*

66

Reservoir

Damside

Crail Museum & Heritage Centre

harbour

West Ness

Ribbonfield

B940

Sypsies

A917

65

Lochton

B940

Tapefield

ruins

Leys Farm

Troustrie

B9171

64 *Caiplie Caves*

Toldrie

Airdrie Farm Cottages

East Pitcorthie

West Pitcorthie

Caiplie

Cornceres

63

Blacklaws

B9131

Cuttyskelly

caravan park

P

Kilrenny

Cellardyke *harbour*

53

3·6 Crail to St Andrews

Distance	13·3 miles 21·4 km
Terrain	pavements, urban and coastal paths, minor road, paths and tracks beside golf courses, cliff-edge and shoreline paths with steps, beaches, paved paths
Grade	generally flat to Fife Ness, minor rise via Boarhills; marked undulations for 2·5 miles, then level before descent to St Andrews
Food and drink	Crail, St Andrews
Summary	the most challenging and remote section of the Path pivots around a dramatic change of outlook at Fife Ness; after a succession of golf courses, it has some rugged coast, and ends at historic St Andrews

Crail   Fife Ness   Kingsbarns   High tide alert   St Andrews

○———————●———————Ⓟ———————△———————○
   2·5/4·0   3·6/5·8   5·4/8·7   1·8/2·9

> ⚠ **Plan your departure time carefully to ensure safe passage at two sections that at high tide are underwater – just beyond the 70-mile mark and also from 77 miles. See page 13 for tide information.**

- Walk down Shoregate and take the first left, then bear sharp right. Turn left along Nethergate to a T-junction. Turn right towards the shore then keep to the seaward side of open space above Roome Bay.

- The path leads up briefly then down again. Walk through a caravan park then a holiday park; opposite Cottage 89, bear right along a path closer to the shore.

- A few hundred metres further on, you enter the Kilminning Coast Wildlife Reserve: see page 78 for the Scottish Wildlife Trust which runs it. Dog owners note: sheep were grazing here when the route was last surveyed.

- The path leads up and over a clearly defined rock rib. After a rocky stretch, steps take you up to SWT signs about the reserve and about Dane Dyke on which you're standing. The area was raided by Vikings and legend has it that a warrior was buried nearby.

- Beyond a large building, return to shore level. The rather rough path leads on below an incongruous modern terrace and the coastguard station, to Fife Ness.

Crail harbour

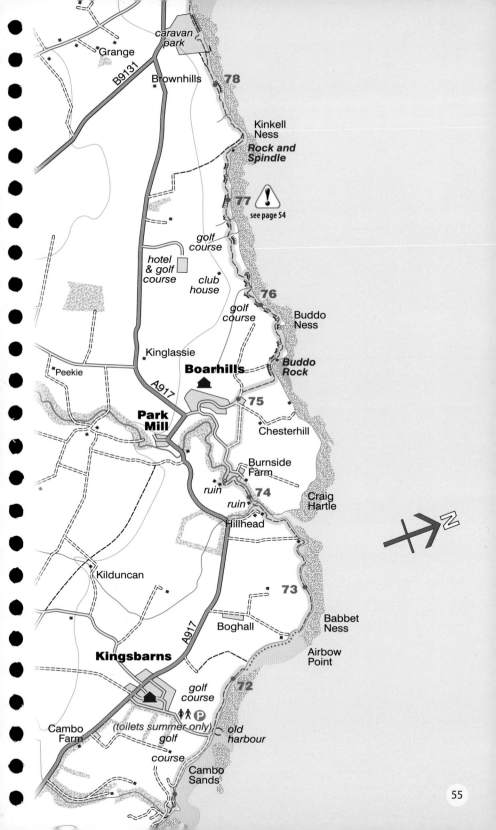

caravan park

Grange

B9131

Brownhills

78

Kinkell Ness

Rock and Spindle

77 ⚠
see page 54

golf course

hotel & golf course

club house

golf course

Buddo Ness

Kinglassie

Boarhills

Buddo Rock

Peekie

A917

75

Park Mill

Chesterhill

Burnside Farm

ruin

ruin **74**

Craig Hartle

Hillhead

Kilduncan

73

Babbet Ness

A917

Boghall

Airbow Point

Kingsbarns

golf course

72

🚻 🅿

(toilets summer only)

Cambo Farm

golf course

old harbour

Cambo Sands

N

Site of the historic harbour at Fife Ness

Fife Ness (headland) is the most easterly point in Fife, with a long association with seafarers' safety. Before modern navigational systems, many ships were wrecked offshore and on the hazardous North Carr Shoals. A buoy was built on the reef in 1809, followed in 1821 by a beacon. More effective lightships provided the service for nearly a century to 1975 when the lighthouse was built. A lifeboat, and later a coastguard station, operated nearby from 1884 until recently.

- Rounding the headland suddenly reveals a breathtaking new outlook – to the north shore of the Firth of Tay and the hills beyond. Here too are a World War 2 lookout and the observatory of Fife Bird Club.

- Continue for 50 m to a minor road, past a small caravan park and a cottage. Opposite is information about the remains of Fife Ness harbour (dating back to the 16th century) and the former coastguard station.

- Follow the route along the edge of a golf course (of Crail Golfing Society, founded in 1786). The stone cottage nearby was Crail lifeboat house from 1884 to 1923. There's an information board nearby about the local legend of Constantine's Cave.

- Walk along the beach to a sign pointing inland; at high tide follow a white-staked path. Beyond the golf course, the path goes between the shore and a fenced field.

The Path beside Balcomie Links

- Cross low cliffs to a stile. A sign directs walkers to the beach for the next half-mile, and at high tide you'll have to wait until it's safe to continue.
- Beyond a rocky beach, cross a stone wall and return to the beach to the next marker. From there you soon join a track; when it reaches a T-junction bear right. (The alternative route signed to the left is useful if the stream is in spate.) Cross Cambo Den.

- Walk past a toilet block (locked at the time of survey). Leave the track to a path on the right at the '16th' sign. This becomes a track and leads past another golf course to a car park. The public toilets here are open during summer only. The road leads inland to Kingsbarns.
- Continuing, you soon skirt another golf course and pass a track providing alternative access to Kingsbarns. Nearby, a sign warns that remote terrain lies ahead and that it's 7½ miles to St Andrews.
- A path leads on near the cliff edge to a sign directing you down to the beach, which you then leave at the end of the sand. Then follow a path beside a field, another beach, rocky shore, more beach and a sign about keeping dogs on leads near horses.
- At a fork, bear right towards Boarhills. The path turns inland beside a stream (Kenly Water). At the entrance to Hillhead, descend to a path. This leads upstream, past an ivy-clad derelict stone building, for about 700 m to a footbridge.

North-west towards Cambo Den

Shore west of Kingsbarns old harbour

- Pass Bankside farm and join a minor road. Follow it for about 300 m to a field-edge track on the right. It leads north-west to a series of clearly marked turns, past a farmhouse, to a grassy track. This takes you towards the shore; past a gate, a path crosses the slope at the foot of low cliffs.

- At the far end of a tiny beach, pass Buddo Rock: see page 16. Continue between the shore and a low cliff, and after about 250 m cross a wall by a stile. Climb stone steps to cross a low cliff, then return to sea level, with St Andrews enticingly in view.

- A narrow path with stepping stones take you across a boggy stretch; then come a string of ups and down on stone steps. Eventually, a short grassy path leads to the longest uphill yet, to another golf course.

Buddo Rock

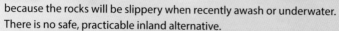

- Shortly, go through a gate and right on a track for about 60 m to a ladder stile, and an easy path. Then, cross a footbridge and descend to a shingle beach.
- Next, you reach a rocky stretch and beyond it a small beach of sand and rocks, signposted 'tidal risk'. If you have to cross at or near high tide, take care because the rocks will be slippery when recently awash or underwater. There is no safe, practicable inland alternative.
- Continue along the beach edge, through a defile and go on above the shore. Look out for the Rock & Spindle formation below: see page 16.
- Beyond another beach, you're back near the cliff-top for a few hundred metres. The track then winds down and around a holiday park near St Andrews. Go down a tarmac path parallel to the beach.
- After about 750 m, cross the lifting bridge at the harbour entrance and turn right. Go up a steep tarmac path beside the cathedral. At a fork, bear left along Gregory Place to reach the town centre.

Ruins of St Andrews Cathedral

St Andrews

St Andrews is one of Scotland's most historic towns. It was once Scotland's ecclesiastical capital, home to bishops and archbishops, and frequented by monarchs. Scotland's first university was founded here in 1413, and it remains one of the most prestigious in Britain.

The town has a modest population (about 15,000) but is recognised worldwide as the home of golf. The Royal and Ancient Golf Club is the international governing body of the sport, and golfers come to play its famous Old Course.

Much of the old walled medieval city survives. Its three ancient streets – North Street, Market Street and South Street – converge on the ruined cathedral.

St Andrews Cathedral was once Scotland's largest church. Its construction began around 1160 and it was dedicated in 1318. Over the years it was extensively damaged by storms and fire. After the Reformation, it was abandoned in 1561, and its stones pillaged for use elsewhere. The site is open all year, and there is a museum in the priory building: see *www.historicenvironment.scot*.

The FCP passes St Andrews Castle ruins on a low headland. The existing structure dates from the 1400s, and it became the official residence of bishops and archbishops in St Andrews. However, it never recovered from severe damage during the religious disputes of the mid-16th century, and by 1700 it was in ruins. The site is open all year: *www.historicenvironment.scot*.

Martyrs Monument

The FCP leaves St Andrews westward, heading for Leuchars, and passes the Martyrs Monument. This commemorates four men who were executed for their Protestant beliefs between 1527 and 1558. Their sacrifice was soon followed by the Reformation of 1560, inspired by John Knox's preaching in St Andrews.

St Andrews Castle

3·7 St Andrews to Leuchars

Distance	6·6 miles 10·6 km
Terrain	consists of flat tarmac paths
Food and drink	St Andrews, Guardbridge, Leuchars
Side trip	Eden Estuary Centre
Summary	from historic St Andrews through pleasant, open countryside, to the Eden Estuary and Guardbridge, then on to Leuchars with its old parish church

St Andrews ● - **Guardbridge** ● - - - - **Leuchars** ●
5·0/8·0 1·6/2·6

- Rejoin the route along East Scores, passing St Andrews Castle and impressive university buildings. After 0·75 miles (1·2 km) pass the Martyrs Monument overlooking the Old Course. Below here, at a T-junction, turn left briefly along Golf Place, then first right along The Links.

- Continue beside the course and turn right at the next T-junction. At a barrier, cross a minor road and bear left along a path beside a car park. You are now on the popular Kingdom Cycle Route – beware of cyclists!

- Go on past the substantial Old Course Hotel, and bear right along the tarmac cycle-way, soon passing the turf-roofed Morris Building. Old Tom Morris (1821-1908) was greenkeeper and professional at the Royal and Ancient for 39 years. He helped to found the Open Championship, struck the first ball in 1860, and won it four times.

- The screen between the cycleway and the adjacent busy A91 starts as a belt of trees, but dwindles to nothing over the next 2 miles (3 km). Several hundred metres beyond Edenside, diverge to a minor road, soon crossing the River Eden on an old stone bridge.

- An information board explains that the stone piers supported a rail bridge, in use from 1852 to 1968. The first crossing was built in the 15th century for pilgrims en route to St Andrews, and survived until 1938. The old paper mill buildings are just downstream from here.

Piers of former rail bridge, Guardbridge

- At the road junction, cross the A919 to follow a path first between houses, then behind them.

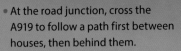
Red Arrows

- For the Eden Estuary Centre, turn right along the A919 for about 200 m to a park and follow the path towards the shore. Contact the Ranger (tel 07985 707 593) for the entry code. This offers superb views of the estuary and is a must for keen bird watchers.

- On the main route, about 500 m from the A919, continue along a roadside path. Cross the Inner Bridge over Motray Water. Pass a small housing estate, and continue beside the A919. Use the pedestrian crossing to reach the road to Leuchars.

- Follow the roadside path, with MoD Leuchars property on the right and soon also on left: see panel. At its northern end, the FCP turns right (east) into Wessex Avenue.

> **i**
> **Leuchars Station**
> The base opened in 1920 as a Royal Naval Air Service airfield. At the beginning of World War 2 a plane from Leuchars was the first British aircraft to engage in combat. Its aircraft specialised in strikes against ships and submarines and in minelaying sorties.
> After 1945 it was involved in reconnaissance and interception of unidentified aircraft. From 1954, helicopters from Leuchars took part in mountain and sea rescues.
> Leuchars air show (2001-2013) often featured the Red Arrows, the RAF's renowned aerobatic team. The station passed to the army in 2015 and is to become the centre of army operations in Scotland.

- Before turning right, continue briefly on Main Street to Leuchars Parish Church, prominent ahead to the left: see below. To reach Leuchars' facilities and refreshments, head west from the church for about 250 m.

- Afterwards, return to Wessex Avenue to resume the Path heading east.

> **i**
> **Leuchars Parish Church**
> This church is dedicated to the obscure St Athernase. Completed in 1187, it is regarded as the best preserved Romanesque (Norman) church in Scotland.
> Its windowless arches around the chancel and apse are at the eastern end, capped by a tower added in the 18th century. The church reopened after major restoration work in March 2018: **www.leucharsstathernase.org.uk**.

Leuchars Parish Church

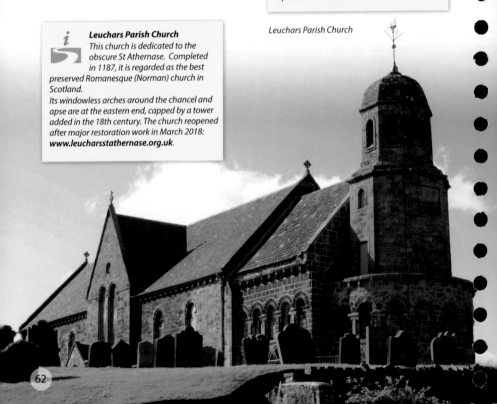

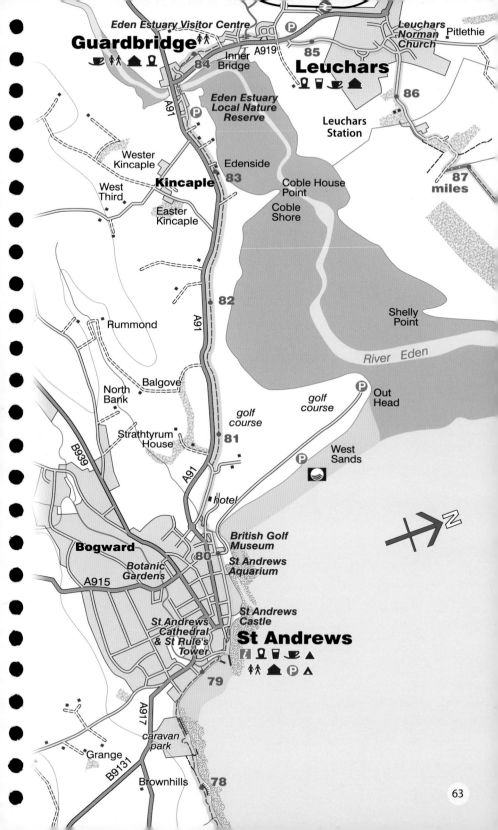

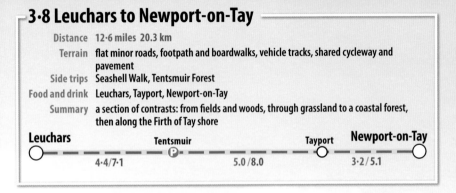

3·8 Leuchars to Newport-on-Tay

Distance	**12·6 miles 20.3 km**
Terrain	flat minor roads, footpath and boardwalks, vehicle tracks, shared cycleway and pavement
Side trips	Seashell Walk, Tentsmuir Forest
Food and drink	Leuchars, Tayport, Newport-on-Tay
Summary	a section of contrasts: from fields and woods, through grassland to a coastal forest, then along the Firth of Tay shore

Leuchars   Tentsmuir   Tayport   **Newport-on-Tay**

4·4/7·1   5.0/8.0   3·2/5.1

- After 250 m, Wessex Avenue reaches a crossroads with Earlshall Road: turn right. Join a path parallel to the road, across an open area. Rejoin the minor road, passing more MoD installations.

- Beyond farm buildings the road becomes a vehicle track and goes through woodland. About 250 m after a right bend, take a path on the left. Fenced at first, it crosses a field, then goes on long boardwalks that keep your feet dry.

- Then comes a pleasant open stretch (about 750 m) of grassland dotted with clumps of birch. Continue along a vehicle track for 1·1 miles (1·8 km) through mixed forest. Go right along a minor road to Tentsmuir Forest car park.

- En route, still in mixed forest, Polish Camp road recalls two Polish army units that were stationed in the area during World War 2. They built the coastal defences, generally on the seaward side of the forest. At the car park, there are picnic tables and toilets, behind which is a useful source of drinking water.

The main Path on Tentsmuir forest road

The Seashell Trail: see map on page 67

At the car park, you have a choice: follow the main Path along its broad forest road, or take the alternative Seashell Trail for the first couple of miles. The forest road is shown in the photo on page 64 and the FCP route is described on page 66.

This page describes the more scenic option. The Seashell Trail comprises two parallel paths with a bridging section: see page 67. Its forest section runs parallel to the main FCP, slightly to its east on lovely paths. Its glorious beach sections offer wide views over Tentsmuir Sands and towards Tenstmuir Point. You can sample both, switching between them by the bridging section, marked by a World War 2 pillbox on the beach.

Whichever parts of the Seashell Trail you use, rejoin the main FCP at the ice house (mile 91·5). You will walk slightly further than on the main Path, but will escape the uninspiring forest road. The Trail runs through a fragile and dynamic coastal area: please tread softly and observe any local signage.

To pick up the Seashell's pale blue waymarkers, walk from the car park/ picnic area towards the coast and head north to where it forks. Bear right for the beach or keep straight on along the forest edge. Once you reach the ice house, resume directions from the middle of page 66.

Seashell Trail inland

Seashell Trail along the coast

The ice house

- Continuing on the main route from the entrance of the car park, bear left along a road which soon becomes a vehicle track leading north. The forest varies in density, and its trees include holly among the Scots and Corsican pines.
- About 100 m beyond a sign on the southern boundary of Tentsmuir Point National Nature Reserve is an ice house, built around 1852 but almost intact. Information boards explain how it worked. It was close to the shore when built, but the coastline has since moved 500 m to the east.
- From here, divert east (along the bridging section of Seashell Trail) for 100 m to reach open ground. This small detour gives an excellent view of the vastness of the Firth of Tay: of all Scotland's large estuaries, this is the most unspoiled.
- Shortly after a track junction on the left (near mile 92) is a March Stone – a pillar about 1 metre tall. It was erected in 1794 to mark a fishing rights boundary (i.e. march).
- About 900 m further on, where the track bends west close to the shore, divert through the trees for about 100 m for another good view of the open expanses of the Firth of Tay estuary. Tentsmuir Point, with its large colony of grey seals, is some distance eastward. The large boulders are World War 2 tank traps.

North towards the Firth of Tay

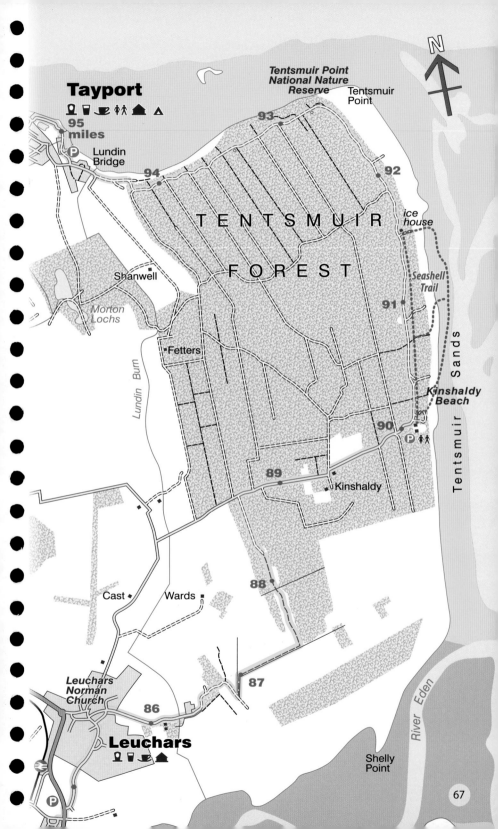

Tayport

95 miles

Lundin Bridge

94

93

Tentsmuir Point National Nature Reserve

Tentsmuir Point

92

ice house

T E N T S M U I R

F O R E S T

Shanwell

Morton Lochs

Fetters

Seashell Trail

91

T
e
n
t
s
m
u
i
r

S
a
n
d
s

Kinshaldy Beach

90

89

Kinshaldy

88

Cast

Wards

87

Leuchars Norman Church

86

Leuchars

Shelly Point

River Eden

- For the next mile or so, note the change in the local topography, as the track winds through a jumble of grassed dunes. At last you come into the open near Tayport Heath, about 4 miles (6·4 km) from the car park. Information boards explain the significance of this valuable natural area and its early history involving the Romans, Picts and Vikings.

- Follow a track to the right to the shore and bear left at the end of the dunes for about 500 m to a road. Either follow the official route (roadside path then first right) or the signposted 'Pedestrian route' through an open area to a car park, where the two routes converge.

- Continue through Tayport Links Caravan Park and back to the shore. Turn right along Harbour Road for about 750 m to the harbour entrance. Go left along a tarmac path.

- Near the western end of the harbour, continue along Inn Street to a T-junction: turn left along a street which soon becomes a path.

- Follow its zigzags up to a street and turn right to a path following the line of a former railway. This leads on for about 500 m, overlooking the firth with two old tall lighthouses below. Continue to the B946 road.

- About 200 m along a roadside path, bear right down to a small car park. Here a Tayport

Old lighthouse near Tayport

Interpretation Board describes the significance of the Tay's natural heritage, and two panoramas identify features across the firth.

- Return to the roadside path, still following the old railway. About 800 m beyond a junction on the left, it passes beneath the towering road bridge. Newport-on-Tay stretches ahead beside the firth, with large 19th century mansions lining the road.

- If this is the end of your walk along the FCP, there are bus stops for services to Dundee along the road, and shops about 800 m along.

Railways in Fife

Parts of the FCP follow or pass close to old railway trackbed, notably near Lower Largo and Tayport. The line into eastern Fife was opened in 1845, reaching Thornton, north of Kirkcaldy. It was extended to Leven, Leuchars, Tayport and, by 1852, it reached St Andrews. In 1857 the line was extended east from Leven to Anstruther and freight trains carried quantities of fish from the East Neuk to farflung markets. Extensions followed during the 1870-80s, e.g. to the Tay rail bridge and from Anstruther to St Andrews.

From the 1950s, the lines became uneconomic and closures followed, leaving no services between Thornton, St Andrews, Leuchars and Newport.

Tayport & Newport

The earliest Tay ferry service plied the firth from Newport, probably in the 1300s. A steamboat pier, designed by Thomas Telford, was completed in 1823.

During the early 19th century, Tayport harbour was busy with whalers. Then in 1847 a roll-on roll-off ferry for the Edinburgh & Northern railway began to operate.

Both towns attracted Dundee's rich industrialists, and their mansions line the waterfront. The beautifully restored late Victorian bandstand in Newport symbolises this era.

From the late 19th century, the rail bridge strengthened Newport's prosperity at Tayport's expense. Finally, in 1966 the road bridge opened and the age of the ferries was over.

Newport bandstand

West across the Firth of Tay from Newport

3·9 Newport-on-Tay to Newburgh

Distance	18·3 miles 29·5 km
Terrain	roadside pavement, field-edge and field paths, farm tracks, woodland and gravel paths, minor roads, farm track, paths and tracks (potentially muddy)
Side trips	Norman's Law
Grade	steady ascent to shoulder of Norman's Law at 260 m/850 ft, with minor ups and downs elsewhere
Food and drink	Wormit, Newburgh
Summary	a distinctive section ranging from residential Tayside up through fields and woodland, then back down to historic Balmerino; after reaching the Path's highest point, it descends through quiet countryside and woodlands to Newburgh

Newport — 5·6/9·0 — **Balmerino** — 4·4/7·1 — **Pittachope** — 8·3/13·4 — **Newburgh**

- Follow the B946 through Newport on roadside paths. At a roundabout after 0.6 miles (1 km) bear right along Boat Road for 300 m, then return to the main road. Continue through residential Wormit, which was the first place in Scotland to be connected to domestic electricity in the early 20th century.

- About 2·5 miles (4 km) from the start in Newport, diverge right down Bay Road. As you pass beneath the rail bridge over the Tay, note the stumps of the piers of its disastrous predecessor.

Tay rail bridge

In February 1878 a bridge across the Firth of Tay was opened, carrying the railway from Wormit to Dundee. Engineer Thomas Bouch's lattice design was lightweight and economical, and at the time, it was the world's longest rail bridge (2 miles/3.2 km).

During a storm force gale on 28 December 1879, 13 central spans collapsed, pitching the train into freezing water. There were no survivors and at least 59 people died. The subsequent enquiry concluded that the bridge had not been built strongly enough to withstand high winds. Its replacement opened in 1887, slightly upstream of the original bridge and parallel to it.

North over the Tay rail bridge

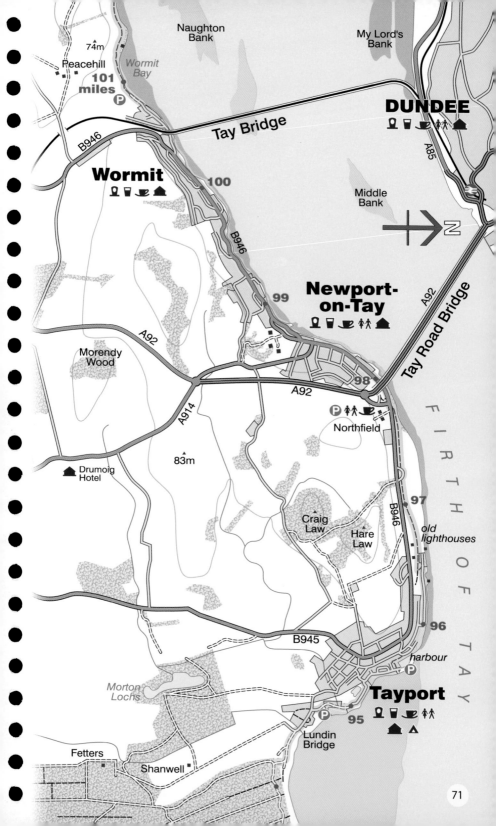

Naughton
Bank

My Lord's
Bank

74m

Peacehill

Wormit Bay

**101
miles**
Ⓟ

DUNDEE
♟ 🍺 ☕ ⚦ 🏛

A85

B946

Wormit
♟ 🍺 ☕ 🏛

100

Middle
Bank

→ N

B946

99

**Newport-
on-Tay**
♟ 🍺 ☕ ⚦ 🏛

Morendy
Wood

A92

A92

98

Tay Road Bridge

A92

A914

Ⓟ ⚦ ☕

Northfield

83m

Drumoig
Hotel

97

B946

*old
lighthouses*

Craig
Law

Hare
Law

F I R T H   O F   T A Y

96

B945

harbour

Ⓟ

*Morton
Lochs*

Tayport
♟ 🍺 ☕ ⚦ 🏛 ⛺

Ⓟ

95

Lundin
Bridge

Fetters

Shanwell

71

- After 500 m the road ends by the shore at a car park. On the far side there's a dignified granite memorial to the Tay bridge disaster, listing the names and ages of the known victims.

- Continue along a concrete path for about 150 m then bear left up a path and follow a series of well-marked field-edge and field paths and farm tracks.

- Exit the fields through a metal kissing-gate into woodland. The undulating path crosses a burn. With the hamlet of Bottomcraig up to the left, the path enters young woodland: look out for roe deer about here.

- The path exits woodland after nearly a mile. Go down steps to a gravel path then soon continue between a large house and the shore.

- A shoreside path leads on to the historic hamlet of Balmerino and you soon come to the Abbey: see panel. This property is very well presented, with various structures (and grassed outlines of others) labelled.

- Follow the road for a short distance from the last house. Turn right along a signed path, at first behind the beach, then following the shoreline briefly. Diverge into the woodland along a path with several bridges.

- Gain height to a field-edge path. Follow it up to a wide track and turn right. Soon, bear left uphill to a junction: turn right along a minor road.

Balmerino Abbey

> **i** **Balmerino Abbey**
> *Established as a Cistercian monastery in 1229, the abbey was completed 200 years later. About 20 monks lived there in 1500, but it was later damaged twice within 60 years. Early in the 17th century the abbey became home for the lords Balmerino until 1746.*
>
> *All that survives is the church's ruinous eastern wall and some associated buildings. The sprawling Spanish chestnut tree here is Scotland's oldest, about 450 years old. Balmerino is cared for by the National Trust for Scotland, and is open year round: see www.nts.org.uk.*

RAIL BRIDGE
IN MEMORY OF
THE PASSENGERS AND CREW OF THE BURNTISLAND TRAIN KNOWN TO HAVE DIED IN THE TAY RAIL BRIDGE DISASTER OF SUNDAY, 28TH DECEMBER, 1879

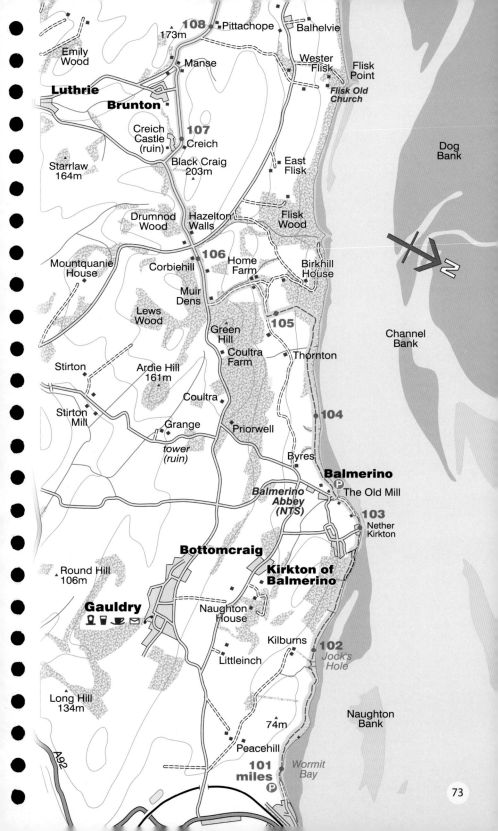

Emily
Wood

Luthrie

Brunton

108
173m
Pittachope
Balhelvie

Manse

Wester
Flisk

Flisk
Point

*Flisk Old
Church*

Creich
Castle
(ruin)

107
Creich

Black Craig
203m

East
Flisk

Starrlaw
164m

Drumnod
Wood

Hazelton
Walls

Flisk
Wood

Dog
Bank

Mountquanie
House

Corbiehill

106

Home
Farm

Birkhill
House

Muir
Dens

Lews
Wood

Green
Hill

105

Thornton

Channel
Bank

Stirton

Ardie Hill
161m

Coultra
Farm

Coultra

104

Stirton
Mill

Grange

Priorwell

*tower
(ruin)*

Byres

Balmerino

P The Old Mill

*Balmerino
Abbey
(NTS)*

103
Nether
Kirkton

Bottomcraig

Round Hill
106m

**Kirkton of
Balmerino**

Gauldry

Naughton
House

Kilburns

102
*Jock's
Hole*

Littleinch

Long Hill
134m

Naughton
Bank

74m

Peacehill

101
miles
P

*Wormit
Bay*

73

- After 700 m continue through the intersection with wide views across undulating fields and woods, dominated by Norman's Law southwestwards.

- At a fork, bear right and pass farm buildings and Creich Castle. Built during the 1550s it was in ruins by 1700.

- A little further on within Creich cemetery are the ivy-shrouded remains of the parish church (dating from the 15th century). At a T-junction near the hamlet of Brunton, turn right.

Creich Castle

- In a lay-by just beyond Pittachope farm buildings is an FCP information board. It explains the game shooting season (from mid-August) when temporary diversions may be signed, the views from Norman's Law and the prevalence of Iron age forts nearby.

- About 50 m further on, go left through a small gate to a farm track. A steady climb leads south then south-west. About 500 m after the bend, a stile over the fence gives access to Norman's Law.

- At 285 m (935 ft) this hill is a worthy detour and viewpoint. You're already at the highest point on the Path on its shoulder, but it's well worth the extra climb (of about 35 m or so vertically) to its summit. Allow 30-40 minutes for the round trip.

Norman's Law

An informal path crosses the field, curves slightly left and up to a stile and gap in the wall. The path rises directly then bears right up to the summit. A location finder on a pillar shows the direction of the numerous hills visible in clear weather, up to 40 miles (64 km) away. Of equal interest to FCP walkers are the Tay rail bridge and the inner Firth of Tay. Retrace your steps to rejoin the main Path.

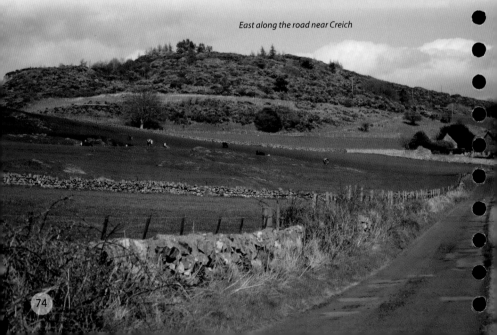

East along the road near Creich

- The track descends steeply through forest and around the slopes of Norman's Law to a gate. Keep to the track, descending generally south-west to a junction: go right towards Briardene. Just past the three cottages, follow the path ahead.

- Within a few metres this leads between a stream and field to an old stone building. Turn right along a farm track. After 500m, at another junction, it's a right turn.

- About 150 m further on, go through a gate into a forestry estate. The track generally gains height up a shallow glen, via a left turn at a fork. After a further 600 m, a small gate opens onto a path, mostly along the woodland edge, across the slope of Glenduckie Hill.

- After about 500 m, the Firth of Tay appears again. Soon the path leads into young woodland and descends through three gates to a field-edge path.

- Continue up to the crest. From here the path leads on between fences; turn right beyond a gate along a grassy track. You are soon rewarded with an inspiring view of the firth and of Newburgh. At the next gate, bear left into some trees, then traverse Lindores Hill.

- Pass two belts of trees and descend on a farm track. Near Old Parkhill go through a gate and bear left, then right down a field.

- Cross a farm track and turn left briefly. At Parkhill, bear right to a minor road where you turn left. After about 50 m, the FCP turns right on a signed path.

- Consider a short detour on the minor road ahead to see the remains of Lindores Abbey and to visit Lindores Abbey Distillery. Opened in 1190, the abbey was destroyed in 1560. Here in 1494 James IV commissioned Friar John Cor to make 'aqua vitae' – the earliest record of whisky production in Scotland. A new distillery with café was built on the farm steading, its stillroom overlooking the abbey, and distilling resumed in 2017 after a 500-year gap. For opening times and visit information, see *www.lindoresabbeydistillery.com*.

Lindores Abbey

- To resume the route, retrace your steps and follow the FCP signed turn (north). The route continues along a stream bank. Follow it past a wooden bridge and bear left along the Firth shore. The open space that you soon pass is the site of the former linoleum factory: see page 19.
- Continue along paths and minor roads to a park opposite Mugdrum Island. Follow the tarmac path, with an information board about the 'Mighty Tay', Scotland's longest river.
- The path soon leads inland. In front of an old building bear left along a path and continue up to a car park. Here an FCP information board marks the terminus – congratulations on completing the Path! For bus stops, a café, shops and pubs, bear left along the main road.

Newburgh

Newburgh was well established by the 15th century when it became a Royal Burgh. The town was once a busy port for the export of fish (especially salmon), also linen, coal and agricultural produce. The linoleum factory was important until it closed in 1980. Nowadays a few boats fish for smelt (a small relative of salmon) during autumn and winter. Local orchards are still plentiful and their produced is sold locally in autumn.

If you have any spare time in Newburgh, you may wish to visit the Laing Museum for its 3000+ antiquarian book collection gifted by local historian Alexander Laing. As of 2018 it was open only on Wednesdays from 12 to 4 pm, but private viewing was possible by arrangement: tel 01334 659 328.

West from the park beside the Firth of Tay

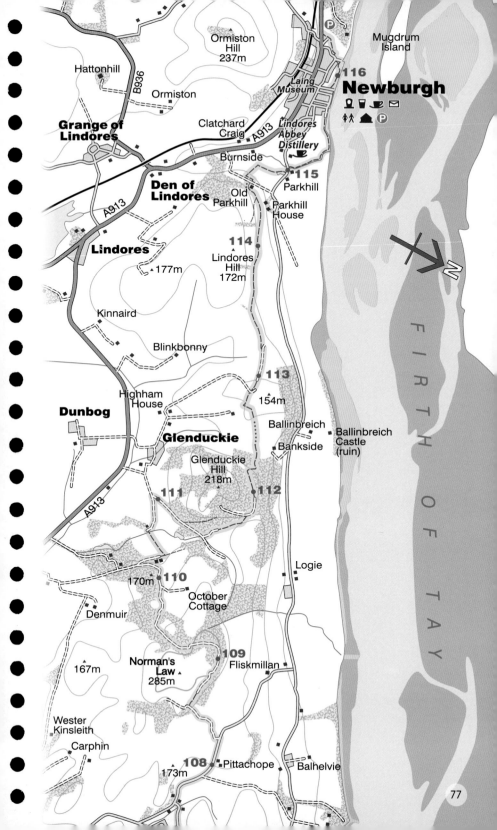

Mugdrum
Island

Ormiston
Hill
237m

Hattonhill

B936

Ormiston

116

Laing
Museum

Newburgh

Grange of
Lindores

Clatchard
Craig

A913

Lindores
Abbey
Distillery

Burnside

115

Den of
Lindores

Old
Parkhill

Parkhill

A913

Parkhill
House

Lindores

114

Lindores
Hill
172m

177m

Kinnaird

Blinkbonny

113

154m

Highham
House

Dunbog

Ballinbreich

Ballinbreich
Castle
(ruin)

Glenduckie

Bankside

Glenduckie
Hill
218m

111

112

A913

Logie

170m

110

October
Cottage

Denmuir

Norman's
Law
285m

109

Fliskmillan

167m

Wester
Kinsleith

Carphin

108

Pittachope

Balhelvie

173m

FIRTH OF TAY

N

4 Reference

Organisations

The FCP is managed, maintained and promoted by the Fife Coast & Countryside Trust, an environmental charity based in the Harbourmaster's House, Dysart:

www.fifecoastandcountrysidetrust.co.uk

The Path was first opened in 2003, with the extensions to Kincardine and Newburgh added in 2011 and 2012 respectively. Visit the Path's official website at

www.fifecoastalpath.co.uk

to find about more about the route and its heritage. Visit its interactive map for points of interest.

Scottish Natural Heritage is a government body that works to care for Scotland's natural heritage. Its website is

www.nature.scot and details of the Scottish Outdoor Access Code are at

www.outdooraccess-scotland.com.

The latter site offers downloads of a pocket guide to the Code and (under *Practical guide for all*) also leaflets for *Dog Owners* and for cyclists – *Off-road cycling: good practice advice.*

The Scottish Wildlife Trust cares for wildlife, campaigns on wildlife issues and develops practical conservation partnerships. It manages three reserves along the FCP: Carlingnose Point, Dumbarnie Links and Kilminning Coast

www.scottishwildlifetrust.org.uk.

The Forestry Commission Scotland is responsible for managing, protecting and expanding Scotland's forests and woodlands:

www.scotland.forestry.gov.uk.

Historic Environment Scotland is the lead body that care's for Scotlands' historic environment including Aberdour Castle, Inchcolm and the castle and cathedral in St Andrews: *www.historicenvironment.scot*. The Fife Coastal Path was recognised by Scottish National Heritage as one of Scotland's Great Trails. For more about the family of 29 such trails, see:

www.scotlandsgreattrails.com.

Web links and accommodation

Visit *www.rucsacs.com/links/fcp* for a comprehensive list of local and specialised websites, including accommodation listings, arts festivals, local history sites and descriptions of the Elie Chainwalk.

Cycling

Cyclists can seek advice from Cycling Scotland (*www.cyclingscotland.org)*, CTC Scotland (*www.ctc.org.uk/scotland*) and Sustrans (*www.sustrans.org.uk*).

VisitScotland website and iCentre

VisitScotland is Scotland's overall tourist organisation. Its website

www.visitscotland.com can be searched for accommodation, places of interest and travel. Its **iCentre** at St Andrews now serves the entire Kingdom of Fife.

70 Market Street, St Andrews KY16 9NU, tel 01334 472 021, open all year.

Baggage transfer and tour operators

Visit our web page for links to companies that offer baggage transfer and inclusive holidays, both guided and self-guided:

www.rucsacs.com/books/fcp

Weather and tide information

The Met Office is the authoritative source for weather information in Britain. Visit their websites:

www.metoffice.gov.uk and
www.metoffice.gov.uk/mobile

Information about tide times is vital for planning your walk. Visit this website for free information at least a year ahead:

www.tides4fishing.com

Notes for novices

For those with no experience of long-distance walking, we have prepared notes on choosing and using gear. Visit

www.rucsacs.com and click *Notes for Novices*.

Transport

For public transport throughout the UK,
Traveline: *www.traveline.info*

For bus, rail and coach services within Scotland:
www.travelinescotland.com

For rail travel and to buy tickets:
www.scotrail.co.uk or
www.thetrainline.com

Edinburgh, Glasgow & Perth:
www.citylink.co.uk

For local bus services:
www.stagecoachbus.com

Edinburgh airport:
www.edinburghairport.com

Glasgow airport:
www.glasgowairport.com

Maps: printed and online

Footprint, which created the maps in this
guidebook, publishes a handy waterproof sheet
map (*The Fife Coastal Path*) consisting of almost
identical mapping at a scale of 1:50,000; in 2018
it cost £6.95, ISBN 978-1-871149-83-8.

Ordnance Survey's Explorer series covers the
route area almost completely at 1:25,000 in
sheets 367 and 371; to complete the final section
into Newburgh you need also sheet 370. Note
that as of 2018, on sheet 371 the route extension
from Newport-on-Tay to Newburgh was not yet
shown, although on sheet 367 the route did
extend to Kincardine. Always seek the latest
editions.

Please visit our online route map at
www.rucsacs.com/routemap/fcp
and zoom in for amazing detail in satellite view.
This shows the extended route accurately and
completely as an overlay on Google maps,
with points of interest. Use it to search for
accommodation and refreshments near the
route.

Further reading

General Guide to the Isle of May James Allan
4th ed (2015) Tervor Publishing, 88pp
978-0-9538191-2-6
Well illustrated guide to the island's geology,
wildlife and history, including the monastery,
wartime stories and details of the lighthouses
and beacons.

The Fife Coastal Path (2012) Fife Coast &
Countryside Trust, 192 pp
978-0-9572346-0-4

The 22 sections of this, the Official Guide, are
written by the Trust's own Rangers who know
the route so well; it contains a mass of local
anecdotes, folklore, detailed information and
photographs, with a welcome from 'famous
Fifers'.

Fife (2008) Liz Hanson and Alistair Moffat
Deerpark Press, 176 pp 978 0-95419-795-7
This large-format hardback has 200 superb
photographs by Liz Hanson supported by a
well-written short history by Alistair Moffat
and makes good background reading.

Pronunciation guide

Aberdour aber-**dow**-er
Anstruther pronounced as spelled, except by
some residents who say **ain**-ster
Culross   **koo**-riss
Kirkcaldy ker-**caw**-dee
Leuchars **loo**-khers
Wormit   **werm**-it

Acknowledgements

The authors wish to thank Simon Phillips of
the FCCT and Rangers Derek Abbott, Deirdre
Munro and Ranald Strachan for answering
our queries and for comments on our draft
manuscript, and also Lindsay Merriman for
proof-reading. We are responsible for any
errors that may remain.

Photo credits

Sandra Bardwell 18, 49, 50/51, 52 (both), 58
(both), 59 (upper), 61, 68, 69 (upper); **Kieran
Baxter** 69 (lower); **British Golf Museum** 20;
Ian Clydesdale title page, 30 (upper), 48
(upper); **Stuart McCandless**/Creative
Commons 15 (upper); **Jacquetta Megarry**
4/5, 10/11 (all), 12 (all), 14/15 (lower), 16 (lower),
17, 21 (upper), 22 (middle), 24 (all), 25, 27, 28,
31 (upper), 33, 34, 36, 37, 38, 39, 40, 41, 42,
43, 44 (both), 45, 46 (all), 47 (both), 50, 51, 56
(both), 57 (both), 60 (upper), 62 (lower), 64, 65
(both), 66 (both), 70, 72 (upper), 74 (both), 75,
76; **David Pritchard** 16 (upper); **Gordon Simm**
22 (upper); **topshotUK**/istockphoto.com 22
(lower). All others are from *www.dreamstime.
com:* front cover *Pitsch22*; back cover and 19
Julietphotography; 21 (lower) *Whiskybottle*; 23
(upper) *Andreanita*; 23 (lower) *Lukas Blazek*; 26
Astar321; 30/31, 32 and 72 (lower) *Sasalan999*;
48 (lower) *Domnhall Dods*; 54 *David Purves*;
59 (lower) *Adam Edwards*; 60 (lower) *Dennis
Dolkens*; 62 (upper) *Andrew Barker*.

Index